Think And Grow To Prosper

Yassine O Oumar

Dedication

I humbly dedicate this book to my elder sister, Nimat Yassine Oumar, who was an inspiration to me and helped me a lot through dark times. She stood by me, shoulder to shoulder, and always listened when I talked about my dreams. Thank you for never discouraging me or letting me down. You are the one who supported me with love and made me believe that anything in life is achievable. I'm sorry that you left us so soon, but your memory will live with us forever.

To my dad, Yassine, who is also my hero. I remember it like it was yesterday how you always supported us mentally, and most often, financially as well. You never gave up on us, especially me. Thank you for disciplining me to be responsible and toughening me up to cooperate with people without exceptions. You could be younger or older, the only advice that stuck on my mind was how I should learn to help people and serve them, and never expect anything in return, I'm glad to have such a hero who worked day and night to make sure that we are safe and happy. It's a blessing to have the privilege to learn from you and put those experiences into practical use today.

To my mother, Ache Youssouf, who stood to be the best mother; she carried me, cherished me, and loved me more than any mother would. Thank you for being a gift to me; you revolved your life around taking care of us. My love for you will never diminish.

I also dedicate this book to every mother around the world.

Acknowledgment

Bob Proctor was my first mentor. I have never met him, but I have kept him on a pedestal in my mind, and he will always be my mentor. My life had shifted dramatically when I locked myself into Proctor's materials, which was about the paradigm shift. My first turning point was the first interview, entitled *"Do you know who you are?"* which was shot in the 70s. That video was the turning point that completely changed my life.

While I could have easily listened to that interview and let it go, I decided to believe his every word because I waited for that time for a little too long. I believe that it was that point where I decided to change my life. I cannot stop thanking Bob for the knowledge that he shared. Bob Proctor is the true master; may God bless you in countless ways!

I would also like to give acknowledgment to Napoleon Hill. I honestly have too much respect for Mr. Hill. His work is immeasurable and priceless; there are no works from any author that compare to Mr. Hill's. He put in over 20+ years of research, even through his darkest moments of defeat. There are only a few people who would be able to pull off the task commissioned to him. He has continued to change lives until today. He is my true hero and a blessing to those who never questioned his work. You are the one who pushed me toward my dreams and showed me how to achieve it.

To Andrew Carnegie, who was also my mentor after Mr. Hill. Never in history has any wealthy individual revealed the secret to his achievement, especially being amongst the billionaires back in the 1900s. Carnegie is the only one who thought about the humankind and believed that procured knowledge must be organized and shared to the world.

Therefore, he believed that, without it, many people would go through life in poverty. By revealing his wisdom to Hill, it turned into the key that drove success from my heart. Even though you passed away a very long time ago, much before even the birth of my great, great grandfather, you still shared your blessings with the world. To Vounneta Tchingonbe Patchanne; I was blessed to be granted with the opportunity of meeting you. You are an amazing person, full of passion. I love how hard working, positive, and passionate you are; your friendship is what I admire the most.

Your limitless vision is what most people need, but very few people have it. Thank you for your support and contribution throughout the time of our friendship.

About The Author

Yassine O Oumar was born in 1987 in Berberati, Central African Republic. He attended his primary to secondary schooling there, then moved to Chad where his parents lived. Soon after getting his high school diploma and pursuing college education in Chad, he immigrated to New York, and after attending the New Jersey City University, he paused his schooling and decided to start a business venture.

Yassine O Oumar gained the inspiration for this book from his mission of self-discovery, and the question of what makes people successful. After years of reading through biographies, he was finally convinced that the answer was within himself. He aims to challenge people who contradict this statement to go on a path of self-discovery and see the results unfold.

Preface

I am a firm believer that success is only a decision away; understanding your goal would dismiss outside forces to control you. Once you understand your mission, you must never acknowledge temporary defeat, or let it knock you off the path that you are on. I guarantee that nothing would hold your success from you. I have personally heard many billionaires speaking and sharing the stories on how they began reaching their goals. They backed their stories with the conviction that made every listener believe that they can achieve it too.

Whenever I hear about anyone who has reached the top and telling their story, I automatically believe it, but the majority of people do not. Life is beautiful, and it is determined by your perception. Since the start of time, there have been only two types of people; the people who have the knowledge, and the ones who don't. The real secret to success is knowledge. In this case, if you want to succeed, then you must need to understand change. Growth is a consistent part of life, and if something fails to grow, it dies. Knowledge is quite similar to that.

Getting through life means that you need to get out of the darkness that consumes you. You can only do that through the light of knowledge. Nowadays, there are a number of ways that you can educate yourself. One of the best ways is to follow one single individual rather than what the majority are doing or saying. This is because most of the people are clueless, have no vision, no hope, no faith, and most importantly, no clear-cut idea about what to pursue. People who force life to get what they want are the ones who achieve their version of success.

These people are often referred to as geniuses, the lucky ones, or simply intelligent. However, the truth of the matter is that none of these individuals are born with those traits. They are, instead, just like everyone else, and this includes you. The only difference is that they made a firm decision to understand themselves and also acknowledge their true power. Through this, their attitude toward life gets better inherently, thereby creating a 'heaven on earth,' which is what God intended for us in the first place. This is why we must adapt to nature's laws, but most of the people aren't aware of them. The naivety of such matters could result in life becoming a major confusion for them, and they can never figure out why.

Ignorance towards the laws of nature can result in diminishing your chances of success. I'm not, in any way, suggesting that I am a genius or a philosopher. However, I have undergone self-discovery and finally concluded that we are the highest creatures that God created. We were given the ability to think, and that is what helps us to create our desired life. Stop and take a look around. Every creature that God created lacks the mental capacity to build a life. Every creature is known to blend in with their surroundings, except for us. We are the only ones who are disoriented because we were given the ability to create the surroundings instead. Unfortunately, the majority of people fail to do so.

My last promise to you is that you can be, and you can do, whatever you want. All you need to do is to hold up a desire for that goal. Take a trip down memory lane, recall your events and circumstances; understand why the events occurred the way they did. It's through this that you will understand what you 'vibrate' through to the universe will happen to you in reality. This will be discussed in further detail in the book. Remember that if you're still struggling, then it's merely because you don't understand your own mind. What you understand from the day you were born was brought to you by your mind. If you tried and you failed, then the evidence would be clear, and you would understand that your method doesn't work. Understand yourself, and your life will come down to you. If you bargain for a penny, then life will not give you any more. Remember to aim higher and keep reminding yourself that your only struggle is in your mind, or what you allow other people to set.

"I do not think that there is any other quality essential to success of any kind as the quality of perseverance. It overcomes almost everything, even nature."

-John D. Rockefeller

Contents

Page Left Blank Intentionally

Chapter 1
Do You Really Know Who You Are?

Life is beautiful, but only for those who understand who they truly are. Most people are wandering around clueless, and those who understand how to define themselves tend to get aggressive when pushed further for an answer. I have talked to many people to understand this strange question, but in the end, I became convinced that nobody is willing, or even beginning to imagine to give me a clear response.

In most cases, understanding ourselves is the most challenging task that we could ever get, and to simplify my statement, it is only through an accurate analysis that we can produce the absolute results. Again, you must pay the price if you really want to succeed, but most people have gotten this concept backward.

You can achieve success through chance. However, the fact is that this world doesn't run on chances, but rather by law and order. This is why the majority of the people are stuck. The big ball of negative energy dominates and gains exclusive control over how they think, decide, collaborate, relate, and get along with others. Breaking that negativity may be challenging but not impossible, mainly since most people have formed a consistent behavior pattern that makes them comfortable. Transforming that into complete bliss is an impossible jump, and that is why getting to know who we are can be petrifying and would require self-discipline.

The question is; how would you define discipline?

In simple words, it's often the ability to give yourself a command and follow it honestly to achieve any goal. Discipline and consistency are the two things that can challenge you and unlock your true potential. However, not everyone wants to pay the price for extended education, simply to become a doctor or make the sacrifice of being an artist.

Life plays no favorites. The law of life is impartial, but only if you can name and claim it to bridge that gap that is standing between you and your dream. Everything that we see was once in mind, whether you admit it or not. Once you can discover who you really are, self-limitation will disappear, and from that point onwards, you will not need validation for your actions.

I have come noticed that 99.9% of people have unclear thoughts that may arise due to stress. To face a change, there has to be a paradigm shift, which transforms the feelings of doubts, superstition, anger, and hate into love, romance, and enthusiasm, etc. This will help people to begin toward a life of prosperity and happiness.

Take this, for example; if I were to ask you when was the last time you ate, your answer would be every day, right? It's important to understand that your mind needs to feed as well. While you may be feeding your body, your mind remains starved, and this can only be taken care of through learning new information. Success can only come to you once you take it step by step and by having a clear cut idea in your mind about how you want to proceed.

Then, and only then, can you read accordingly and move ahead with what you're willing to do. Remember, leaders are always readers, and this is the reason why the ladder of success is never crowded at the top. The calling is yours; it's up to you to decide whether or not you are willing to climb higher. It's never a smooth start and will definitely come with a price. So it's vital that you start small by reading a page every day, if you are able to do it repeatedly for a month, you need to keep up the consistency.

It all begins with the right frame of mind, which will later turn into action, and then a habit, and soon it will become a part of your character, ending in your inevitable destiny. You will look back and be grateful to yourself for taking action first. The essence of who you are is that you are a spiritual being with intellect and live in a physical body. In other words, you are a mass of energy, and you function on a frequency.

The fact of the matter is that the sole responsibility of change is yours, and this dictates how much you're willing to learn and grow. Real magic comes from self-discovery, which is a power that can change the world. Deciding to read and learn with a target of just 30 days can immensely alter your destiny and make you the captain of a smooth sailboat going for success. Changing the concepts in your mind can ultimately result in changing your destiny.

The system today is controlling the majority of the people, instead of using their will power to control themselves and block all negativity of thoughts that flow their way. Without self-awareness, they simply let the media do their thinking for them without understanding the kind of power they possess, which can counter or reject ideas. Unfortunately, they allow people's opinions to be called facts and thereby be accepted. The lack of self-discovery can break the laws of the universe unknowingly and result in ignorance. It's only through knowledge and curiosity that you can make a decision and create your reality. While you may question your skills and education, it's essential to know that, to change your fate, you need to simply use your mental drive to gain the knowledge you need.

However, before moving on, it's important to understand what education is. The Latin word, 'Educo' derives education, and it means to induce, draw out, or develop from within. Let me clear this up; an educated person is not necessarily the one who has an abundance of general or specialized knowledge, but rather the one who can develop the higher faculties of their mind in any situation.

They can get anything they want without violating the rights of others. Thus, this line defines clearly what education is. The question that will come into most readers' minds is, *"what are our higher faculties?"* Well, they are your will, imagination, intuition, reason, memory, and perception. To shape your future, you must be willing to alter the old conditions of your habits and change your life, not by fighting it, but by building a new design while making the existing one absolute.

There was once a time that I personally didn't like to read; it was only when I underwent self-discovery that incessant thoughts started entering my mind. Some of these thoughts were negative, and some were positive, but all together, they showed me the evidence on how I was affected. It was then that I made up my mind and decided to immediately shut off the flow of all negativity by controlling my thoughts. It was only then that I was able to create my reality.

I didn't know how to, but I believed it and monitored my behavior daily and eventually, noticed a change. I had also read that I must take full responsibility, and only focus on one thing at all times, which meant I needed to focus on the positive aspect constantly. When I felt the alteration of my old self take place, my mind couldn't comprehend what was taking place.

However, I knew that a decision had to be made, and it was made; to read and listen to audio books every day. The efforts of authors in any type of book can revolutionize your world and change your destiny. I have seen many motivational speakers state that one book changed the whole course of their life. However, while that may be true, you need to know whether or not you are self-aware and have developed enough confidence to meet the challenges and be confident about overcoming them. If it's not and you're not sure enough, then my suggestion would be to immerse yourself entirely inside books, especially inspirational ones. Once you start, you will realize that there is a chemical rush in the body that would push you more toward reading. Once you get all the toxicity that is claiming your mind, you will not only feel safe and confident but also find that all the negativity will immediately leave your mind.

It's crucial to understand that the mind will only accept one thing at a time; either the positive or the negative, knowledge or ignorance, and you must make up your mind and take control over your life. If not, you will face the circumstance that the Bible refers to; a warning that tells you never to consider the opposite. That means you should never ask for what you don't want.

"Ask, and you shall receive. Knock, and it shall be open unto you. Seek and you shall find, for everyone that asked has received."

The question is, are you ready to ask? I believe everyone on this planet has a gift, and it's your job to inquire about it. Once you receive it, you will have to make up your mind to act upon it as your duty. Often, once the mind is clear of all the stress, you will be able to see clearly and start going up the ladder without anyone questioning how you started. It takes a lot of courage, persistence, discipline, decision, enthusiasm, and faith to get where you have to. Not everyone is willing to pay the price to procure all these traits of character; so I hope that you will get to this level, because if it's meant to be, then it's up to you.

It's also essential to keep in mind that you have a choice to pick which aspect you want to focus on, and thus determine if you wish to choose knowledge or ignorance. Most people say knowledge is power, but that is not true; knowledge is power only when used or directed through a plan to meet definite ends. The problem with most people is the lack of decision and dismissal of their current condition. However, it's all about the lack of techniques, even though it's effortless.

If you don't like your result, you must change the way you think and begin developing a new neural pathway, so you can break up the old habit which works against your benefit. I believe all the habits you have now are not serving you for your interest, and my most significant challenge for you is; what is your willingness to learn and what is your willingness to accept change. You must be high on both; otherwise, you are wasting your time. Before deciding on giving up, consider giving a thought to these two statements, and if you're ready, it will be your job to describe your favorite things that you loved and replace that with books or audiobooks. Secondly, it's essential to understand your willingness to change; giving up on eating unhealthy food, laziness, playing, wasting time, and instead, devoting your time to reading.

Not only that, but you must also change the way you think, which is vitally important because if you continue to think like you always thought, you will continue to get what you always got. Many people usually mention how they would give up on their routine and change, but end up dismissing it. In this case, the trick is not to choose a variable and completely diminish the other. The facts of the matter are that you must have a high willingness to learn and to accept change.

To climb the ladder of success, you must first change and be reborn again mentally, spiritually, and physically, by forgetting all the past to start with a clean sheet of paper with no hate, no superstition, and no jealousy. Instead, you should have love and ready to serve the world. We all know that we are creatures of habits, and there is no difference between people when you get past culture. When talking about the potentiality of human beings, let your mind go back to a hundred years ago, to understand the extent of what we have accomplished today. We can fly higher than the birds, swim faster than the fishes, and all these achievements come from only one source; it's the mind. It's now your turn to say that you're going to change your world from now on, regardless of the hurdles in your path, simply because you will be working with a power that works in an orderly manner.

People that have changed the world today had a vision, faith, persistence, and imagination, and the fact that they refused to let the outer world control them. You must decide to change and learn new things, along with updating your knowledge on successful people, such as inventors, industrials, and doctors and follow their footprints to become much like them.

Having a role model to emulate is the key to success, especially since you can relate to their life struggles and learn from them to reach where they have gotten. However, one of the most crucial factors to look into is defining your happiness. Some people believe that it is possible to purchase happiness by currency value, but I'll have to disagree to that. Reaching a position of success and gaining money cannot determine your happiness. Instead, happiness is the state of mind which can be developed by ourselves. 98% of the population is said to have the same mentality, which is why they cannot rise beyond mediocrity. That means the poverty of consciousness is a pure disease that affects most people and prevents their success from occurring.

Take, for instance, the life of students. They become mentally invested in their education and might end up with dire consequences if they don't meet their goal. What this means is that it is relatively significant to entertain your habits but not let the pattern control you to the extent that it keeps you from achieving true success and happiness. Keeping in mind that education is not the definition of your future, you already have the tools needed to bring it to the surface.

True power is basically energy, which discusses how everything is created to transform. You can learn from your mentors and use their mannerisms, examples, and lives to learn right from wrong and analyze every statement and opinion before accepting it. Your life will only transform once you're ready, and while some would be ready, others aren't. Think about it; would you rather be a guy who lived on the safe side in his youth, only to reach 70 years old and on a wheelchair and begin thinking about all the missed opportunities? Timing can be everything, and God has given each of us different gifts, which we need to handle. Remember, the tools will unlock the master key to riches, and through them, you can educate yourself and adapt yourself to the laws of nature. You can easily profit by them, or else you might end up getting hurt because the laws do not deviate, and you cannot stop yourself from their energy.

As mentioned above, everything is energy, and that means your thoughts are energy as well. Every time you think, you are transmitting energy, and if you do not know what you put out, they may come back to you. It's crucial that you avoid making this mistake and not discover these laws because they are vital to success. All you have to do is dedicate yourself to studying, and you will only get one thing as a reward. Remember; as you sow, so shall you reap.

Be smart and cut yourself from the average people, who talk about limitations and steal your dream. Stand up and seek knowledge about yourself and your capability. Schools do not define who you are and whatever program that you had controlled your life, behavior, and decisions. Your will power is your determination, and that decides how far you can move ahead. Nothing is impossible if you know just what you're willing to opt for. Think about the battle that took place at the moment of your conception; millions of sperms had participated in a battle, and only one had won, and that was you. So you're not here by accident, you are here because God decided and successfully executed a plan for your existence to come into this world. I believe this recognition would have an impact on your life. All you have to do is not to doubt it because when you are in doubt, you're sending a vibration to your creator that your existence is by luck. It's time that you stood up and accomplished what you were brought here for.

Statistics show that over 50% or more Americans go to jobs they hate. It's a given that you cannot be successful in something that you hate. Look around and see all of today's billionaires and ask them what the secret to their success is. I bet you had the answer in mind already; you must love what you do, even if you're working 15 hours a day.

Your work should be fun for you, which, by doing that, you learn who you are, and that's how great ideas can come to you, and you will know that this is it. Again, 99.9% of the stress or negativity must be vanished, and that can only be done by reading books and listening to motivational audio books. You can turn this into a new routine, and whether or not you like the routine, you will have to do it, and sooner or later, your skepticism will be replaced by belief. Only then will you be taking off like a rocket! Whenever you do something that you do not like, and when you decide not to ask for guidance, remember; seek and you shall find. To do or have anything requires a sense of direction, which most people do not have. It's quite similar to when the boat is about to leave the harbor, and the captain talks about the precise time and destination of the ship. Human beings, while knowing their destination, it's crucial that they think and get a clear picture of where they're going.

I remember when I was listening to one of my favorite mentors, and he stated that only 2% of people think, 3% of people think that they think, and 97% of people rather die than think. It's something that got me wondering how this statement is astonishing and staggers the imagination to break this down in the simplest way. It is evident that people are not thinking because of the program, and the program is unclear, which cannot add to one benefit but only detract from. I have seen people that do not have even a high school diploma influencing the entire world, and people with even lesser education becoming inventors and transforming the world with useful services. People with meager education can't read and write, but when they discover who they really are, they became unstoppable. For them, they are able to keep climbing the ladder of success and stay there. It isn't difficult, but you must take that first step and think like a scientist trying to find a cure to the outbreak of a virus. There are so many problems that are waiting to be solved. Are you ready to participate in the race, or are you happy where you are, with a limited lifestyle and the lack of real joy? It's essential to remember that just getting by is not true success.

You need to dream a little bit and forget your past. It helps to think about your future and everything that you have to achieve. The past is not changeable, and thinking about it is merely equivalent to planting the seed of something you do not want. By focusing on your past ailments, you tend to get exactly that. Who you are now is entirely different from back then, and you need to focus your energy on choosing to move yourself to the opposite side of the scale. As far as you're concerned, you only have one life here, and you do not know when you will leave this planet, so why not starting loving people, helping them, cherishing them, and caring for them? Hence, what you will get in return is abundance from an infinite source of supply.

Have you ever considered thinking about the abundance that you have for free? Well, we do, and we take it for granted and never give a thought to it. We have plenty of fresh air, the abundance of water, the abundance of food, millions of types that you can choose from, the abundance of trees, and the list keeps on going on. This is the infinite source of abundance that I'm referring to, so the happiness is yours and you must feel good at all times when thinking about everything mentioned above.

At this point, you should be thankful that no matter what happens in your life, it can either be bad or good. Your statement should remain as *"I'm happy and grateful."* This is true, even if you're about to file bankruptcy, going through a divorce, or you lose someone you love. Your first mission is to feel good all the time.

"Aim for the moon. If you miss, you may hit a star."

-W. Clement Stone

Chapter 2
Are You Willing to Pay the Price And Discover the Magic within You?

For most people, winning in life roughly equates to using a shortcut. Anything that you do has the tendency of coming back to you, but that's mainly dependent on your perception. However, before understanding that, it's essential to get one thing straight; who is your role model when it comes to chasing your dreams? This question is important because, if you fail to have a mentor, you're necessarily on the road to losing while making a conscious effort to succeed.

This is because following your dreams and goals means that you have to understand how you can move ahead truly. This is best understood by the trial and error method that your role models have already gone through. Not just that, these people live the life that you envision and so, looking at their reality can motivate you to make it yours. I used to have a friend whose father worked at USPS. As we were talking one day, he started discussing his dad's business and said that, regardless of the hard work, he was still struggling financially. My friend decided to take matters into his own hands and put an end to his father's troubles. There was one thing that he said which stuck to me;

"We live in the world's most powerful country, where everything is abundant. Then why do we have to live from paycheck to paycheck?"

He mentioned that people who were the same age as his father had come into the country with no opportunities awaiting them but eventually succeeded. His father, however, didn't make it as far, but my friend knew that it didn't mean he wouldn't either. He developed an awareness because he realized the truth of life; that success is his birthright, along with joy, love, and peace of mind.

This recognition is the key to success. It was from then that my friend automatically developed the strength and faith to succeed. What concerned me, however, was when he asked whether there was a book about reaching success from absolutely nothing. He aimed to get it and reach somewhere from nowhere. He looked at stories of people, and how they achieved success. He learned from them and their mistakes.

He has more than 2,000 books in his apartment today. My friend has changed and made his way to the ladder of success all by himself. His story further made me believe what people actually need the most is awareness. He decided to burn all the bridges and cut all sources for retreat, which was vital for success. This further proves how important it is to have a role model who shows the failures, as well as the achievements. It also incites your ability to move forward.

Now, one of the biggest problems that most people have is that they decide to remain in their comfort zone, regardless of whether or not they are happy with their current situation. All you need to realize is that we have one lifetime, and it's our duty to make it worthwhile. Self-discovery can help you reach that potential. It is one of the most critical recipes that you can own.

What you have in you is mind-blowing, and once you go on the journey to understand yourself, you can face the rewards of what comes next. Nevertheless, in order for that to happen, you need to look at your surroundings and change your friends' circle. The moment you start to discover who your real friends are, the circle immediately shrinks while better friends start to enter it. As stated earlier, your income is the average of your closest friends combined.

One of the best examples I have is about a friend of mine back in high school. While he was busy missing his courses and hanging out, we were busy studying. I had tried to make him understand countless of times to focus on his education, but it was all in vain. He had heard me, but never really listened, which means that my words never really got absorbed into his brain. Now, we had the department of scholarship, which was organizing a midterm to test students who were talented enough to be rewarded overseas admission for further studies.

This opportunity came in the form of an examination, and while everyone else was granted the scholarship, my friend was left behind. The bottom line is that, while a good break does appear in our daily lives, we need to be prepared to grab the chance that may have presented itself only once in a lifetime. It's only the people who are prepared that will get the opportunity.

But what does it mean to be prepared?

Well, it means to read and take control of your thoughts. Ideally, it means to keep your focus on your goal. Here, your thoughts represent how inclined you are to reaching your potential. Controlling your thoughts will make everything fall into place. The only thing that every person has exclusive control over is their thinking. The ability you hold to control your thoughts is a gift from the Creator, which only a few people know and understand. By controlling your mind, you can control your destiny here on earth. The problem with the majority of the people is that they tend to block their minds to the possibility of what could be. Even clear-cut evidence can be termed as impossible for them.

A great example here could be the law of gravity, which states that what goes up, must come down – when you walk up a building and stand on the edge, then you will come down. This is regardless of whether you believe in gravity or not. The reality of life is what a man's thinking can make of it; powerful observations can create influential results.

Man is considered to be the dominating creature since the very beginning, simply because of our power of thought. This wasn't an accident, but rather a set of subsequent events which proved that we are connected to our Creator. Both science and religion agree that nothing new can be created or destroyed; it's merely transformed. Looking at every creature, including cats, dogs, snakes, and lions, it's evident that their thinking ability did not evolve. The evidence is quite clear. To be a great scientist, one must be curious and go above and beyond in their thought process. The ability to think acts similar to dynamite; if it's not organized and directed through a practical plan, then it will destroy the only hope of success. To be an accurate thinker, one must learn by disclosing their weakness, call attention to it, and get it eliminated. The fact of the matter is that many men do not know where the power of a human being is located. This is primarily due to a lack of knowledge.

Knowledge is the crux that builds a person's ability to act. The mind should be able to recall the information that is required for use. For example, just as a man cannot fix a car without the appropriate tools, knowledge holds an even more serious side to it. Even if we decide to supply all the necessary tools, one cannot detect or discover the issue of the automobile without experience or examination.

By looking from a practical standpoint, every single move will contribute to your success. Let's take a look at engineers when they decide to build a skyscraper, and the first requirement is to build the foundation, which has to be deep, or else nothing will last. Knowledge is like that foundation which builds the skyscraper from the ground up.

It's essential to understand that learning is equivalent to earning, the earlier you learn; the better it will be. Instead of wasting time and procrastinating, it's crucial to work on gaining a high willingness to learn and to accept change. While knowledge is important, what needs to be taken into a much deeper consideration is surrounding yourself with people, who can show you who you truly are. Owning knowledge is not enough; you need someone to show you what you possess.

Nature is power; just like a farmer who wants to plant a crop in the ground, what would be the first requirement? Well, the soil has to be prepared before planting. Once the plantation is done, the final result will come from the farmer. Actually, no! Nature will take care of the rest and reward them in abundance. The job of the farmer is only to harvest at the right time. When one takes the first step, the rest automatically falls into place.

It helps if you start searching for meaning; mainly questioning the purpose of your life. Many people don't know why they are here, while very few people do. Those who do, have an extraordinary life and unfortunately, for those who don't, they always justify why they couldn't. Sometimes, they also condemn those who had risen themselves above the crowd. Instead of searching for life's truth, people tend to rely on media to guide their thoughts and actions. One of the main things that media promotes is the idea of working hard, rather than working smart. It shows that success cannot be achieved, unless and until you labor hard and see the sweat of your eyebrows. What you can do, however, is reject the idea and never accept the falsehood of this statement. A simple example can be of construction workers who are the hardest working individuals, and yet, they don't make enough money to be considered as being even close to wealthy.

All through history, wealth has been found to land in the hands of people who used their imagination and thinking power to create items that sustained the world. People with such attitude often are not and cannot be stopped by circumstances or surroundings. If you want to control a situation, you must first be able to gain control over yourself. It's not about how successful individuals lack problems. The fact is how they choose to act or solve their problems and continue to grow. It's vital for us to observe the ever-growing world with an open mind, and notice how it would be without the technological advancements of today.

The people who do are the ones who don't allow anyone to stand in the way of their personal initiative. They have a clear understanding of their goals, and thus are able to make an informed decision on how to proceed with their ideologies to the final destination. Once they've reached their potential, they are able to enjoy the work and continue to persist and get ahead. This is one of the main reasons that we can live in a world of technological advancements and luxury. It's because of the work of people who failed and yet, never gave up.

To reach the top of the empire, the same ideology must be followed by those who are willing to bring their views forward. You need to understand that your life begins each day with a blank canvas; what you put on it is entirely up to you. Life is quite like a movie, and most of us tend to keep replaying that movie again and again, without owning the ability to stop. Sooner or later, you'll see the crux of the movie align in front of you, and you need to make sure that it's genuinely worth watching. The magic ingredient to receive that is to block out the dark cloud that fogs your mind.

Anyone who tries to break the divine pattern that has been established by the universe will go through this life in poverty because no creation can replace the laws of the universe. On the other hand, one may benefit from them by adopting the right attitude toward life. Take a child as an example. When they are born, they are mainly influenced by their surrounding; both negative and positive. It shapes the person they are bound to become. As an adult, however, they have more control over their mind and can take control of their desires.

Our first duty is to connect to the power within ourselves; that power is the cause of all the evolution of human beings. You cannot rely on anyone to show whether or not you can succeed. You have to believe in yourself and your own ability. People don't succeed by chance, so you must pay the price. If you trick yourself by waiting for a savior to come and rescue you, then you are sunk. It's the same as how you cannot put the price tag on fish while they are still in the water. Your success requires many steps, but you cannot get it done until you make the decision to begin the first step.

As I was driving to downtown New York on a beautiful day, I saw a post which stated that in 1909, a 71-year-old had walked from New York to San Francisco in 104 days. That post shocked me because it requires the self-discipline of a higher degree. Ask yourself, as I did, *"would you be able to challenge that?"* Perhaps not, but the point that I'm trying to emphasize on is simple; first you must define what you want and the lengths you would go through to get there. Back in the day, when I used to be a cab driver in New York, my most frequent customers were students. Some of them loved chatting because they felt bored. Out of curiosity, I asked many of the students if they really know who they are.

A student who was enrolling in four years at university couldn't answer this fundamental question because nobody taught them anything about themselves in school. This is a fact, it stated that you could take ten people aged 20 and the time they reach 70, and only one will be rich while two others would be financially independent. Three of them would still be working, and the rest of them would be broke. This is because they lack a goal or an idea to work towards. Usually, you set a goal that will control your thoughts, and when your goal is big enough, it will automatically pull you toward it. In order to get somewhere, you need to follow the 3% of people who accumulate 97% of the world's riches. Take a good look at these three strategies for earning;

- One is called work for money; which means that you must go out and earn money. It is termed as generating an active income. If you don't show up, there is no gain. This strategy is known to be the worst and yet, and it is chosen by most people.
- The second strategy is investing; your money will generate a profit for you. The worst case scenario in this is that 97% of people do not have money to invest and use this strategy.

- The last approach is where you create useful service to others, and the money comes in, whether you're working or not. You can only use this strategy when you discover the truth about yourself. This category belongs to special people who have the enthusiasm, love, tolerance, faith, persistent, and patience to get there. The only secret is to discover who you are and never stop studying because new ideas tend to get blocked from reaching you.

Your mind is mainly full of irrelevant information that blocks your ability to succeed, even if the opportunity presents itself. If you are ready to discover whether or not you need to be true to yourself, then you have to make a commitment that you will study and keep learning until the very end.

It's vital to get out of your conditioning and start moving forward. A simple example of conditioning is how people who get out of jail tend to return to it because of their old habits. Change can only occur once you change your thoughts. Changing your behavior and the ability to grow can only happen through your mind.

"Set a goal to achieve something that is so big, so exhilarating that it excites you and scares you at the same time."

-Bob Proctor

Chapter 3
What do You Really Want

Desire creates the starting point for all the achievements that you want to attain. My mentor once pointed out in a seminar that getting what we want is never the issue; however, making the decision is where the problem lies. Since the very beginning, every accomplishment was based on desires or goals. Throughout history, the people who reached their potential and got through their goals were those who were determined to achieve them. Without it, it's quite difficult for someone to grow.

However, before going further, it's essential for me to clarify some scientific facts, so you can embrace your own true power. At the turn of the century, both Thomas Edison and Albert Einstein had agreed that the brain was the broadcaster, as well as the receiver, of good and bad thoughts. When you release a thought vibration, it's then picked up by the other brain, and then it affects all physical matter. I'm quite sure that you must have experienced this reality, which is referred to as coincidence.

An example could be when you have an urge to call someone, and suddenly, you are receiving an incoming call from that person. Little do we know that the thought waves are cosmic waves that penetrate time and space. To understand this well, we need first to know the laws that govern our lives. One of these laws is the law of vibration, which states that everything is continuously moving, and nothing is at rest. Wherever you are, look around you; while you may not be able to see it, everything is vibrating. We, as human beings, think on frequencies. When you think, your mind flips to a different frequency, and when you transmit those thoughts over a long period, it comes back to you.

Nothing occurs by chance. Going back to my youth; when I was growing up, I used to be obsessed with the USA. I would continuously talk about traveling to America all the time. My parents had immigrated to Central African Republic, where I was born, and I spent my entire childhood there. After high school, my dad had decided to send me to his homeland. Although I didn't know why, but I concluded that I would go back to my parent's homeland for my further education. When I arrived in Chad, I was told to learn English, and so, I decided to register myself at the American Language Center, ALC.

I took an admission test and passed, then started from level 2 to get TOEFL. I knew that it would take two years, and once I had accomplished it, I was awarded a certificate. Now, I had everything clearly planned out; I would get the certificate, apply for a student visa, and then pursue my education in the U.S. I became obsessed with learning, and my desire was always in front of me. Overall, it was driving me day and night to reach my goal.

After I joined the ALC, I discovered another activity that was going on. It was a club where I was introduced for the first time. Since I didn't know how it worked, something told me that I should give up, but my teachability index was always before my eyes. This index shows just how much I'm willing to learn. However, the actual factor that pushed me toward it was what I had promised myself before; I would do whatever it takes to learn English, no matter how many challenges I would have to surmount.

Honestly, I did not know what I was doing, but I was scaling great heights in all my activities. I was getting good grades, passing with "*A*" in all my classes, and I was spotted early by the club staff and became part of them. The funniest thing is that, by aiming high, I became confident in myself. Soon after, I met a guy by the name of Alhadj, and we became friends. Our friendship was tremendous, we were talking about the same stuff stated in another way, and we were on the same frequency. One of his dreams was to come to the USA too. I used to work in a shop and sell motorcycle parts, which was part-owned by my older brother, Bachar. My friend was a photographer working with his uncle. Time passed to six months away from my TOEFL graduation. It was a quiet morning when we headed to the internet café.

My friend, however, detoured saying that he had a goal to work on. I took a work station next to him and asked what he was doing. He then told me about the DV lottery. He said to me that it's a system which is created by the U.S federal government, where they select around 50,000 people each year, at random, to be admitted into the U.S. I was so excited about that news; it was like an answer to all my prayers! It was a dream come true.

We immediately took a photo, filled up the application, and submitted it on October 20th, 2009. If I got randomly selected, then I would be in the U.S by 2011. Back then, while I had a Yahoo account, I hardly ever used to check it. One night, I had a strange dream. I dreamed that I was being told to go and check my mail. When I awoke the next morning, I could still hear the command clearly. I was a firm believer that it could be a blessing. So I prayed, I took my breakfast, and went to work. After a couple of hours, my brother decided to send me to the market, and on my way there, I remembered my dream, and on my way back, something again hit me. Something told me not to pass the internet café, and I knew I had to listen and follow it. Once I went inside and logged on, I saw the email that I was waiting for. It was like magic! It read, *"You have been selected randomly in the DV lottery for the session 2011. This email is coming from the Kentucky Consular Center (KCC)."*

I still couldn't believe it. I quickly printed out the page, called my friend, told him all about the miracle, and enthusiastically broke the news to him. He said that he couldn't believe it until he saw it, so I exited right away and went directly to his apartment. We read the page almost ten times in a row until we were convinced that this was it. I do believe that there is a power that responded to our prayers, and that is a fact. While joining as a club member, one of my music class teachers, Kidjang, became my friend. Kid was one of the good guys and a really great teacher. What I admired the most about him were his simplicity and positivity. Kid had gone through a similar process and had fulfilled all his documentation as well. So when we received the letter, something told us to contact Kid. Once we did, Kid was quite helpful, and after we double checked with him, everything was clearly highlighted. I did the process and sent the required documents back to the U.S. By now, my imagination was on fire, and I literally saw myself already in the U.S. My mood was automatically uplifted, even before the approval. After my case was processed, I received an interview letter in the box.

The challenge here was to travel from Chad to Cameroon because the U.S embassy in Chad did not issue immigration visas. I decided to go there, and my uncle welcomed me to his house. Surprisingly, Kid was in town and was impatiently waiting to be called to pick up his visa. The day of my interview arrived, and early in the morning, I prayed because I could already see myself in possession of my visa. I checked in with the security where a quick check was done, and my name was on the sheet paper for the interview.

I did the necessary tasks, and then I was called in. I stepped in with a feeling of confidence, gave a quick introduction with a smile, and waited. I can recall that moment as if it happened yesterday. The officer asked me two questions; the first was, do you know anybody that lives in the U.S? My answer was yes, and then the second question was, *"Your high school diploma is from Chad so, by law, we need to run a check to see if your diploma isn't fake."* I replied with an affirmative, and then two officers discussed amongst themselves and then said, *"I'm giving you the visa, which means that you are approved."* I was absolutely ecstatic! I came back a couple of days after my approval and picked up my visa.

This whole event gave me a firm belief in how the strength of your desire can turn your dreams into reality. The majority of the people do not know what they want, and so, they never get it. If you cannot define what you want, then how would you expect to get it? The truth is that if you don't put the right vibration to the universe, then the universe cannot send it back toward you. I have spoken to some of my friends, and sometimes jokingly, I asked them what they truly want. Some of them would say that they don't want to have cancer. Here, the focus is on the word 'cancer.'

Similarly, someone said that they want to get out of debt. Here the focus is on the word 'debt,' instead of saying that I would like to be debt-free. Again, another one stated that I don't want to be fat, the vibration is 'fat.' This is amongst the biggest problems that the majority of people are facing. People believe that they know everything by tricking themselves that they are on track. The key is knowledge, not ignorance. Some people wouldn't believe that they could achieve success, even if you tell them that they could. In this case, the belief also plays a significant part in determining your success.

The power of intense desire is unexplainable. Back in the day, I used to have a car, an Acura TSX. I had it for a couple of years, and one day, as I was going down the stairs, I thought about how I hadn't yet gotten into an accident, and how it was in good shape. So here, the vibration was 'accident,' and you couldn't believe what had happened next. After a few weeks, I received a call from an old friend who told me that she was going to the club and that I should join her. Even though I was busy that day, I decided to go out with her.

Afterward, I had to drop her to her apartment. I suggested that she stay at my house instead; since I had a bedroom free. She agreed, and as we were heading there, I came across a stop sign and came to a complete stop. I checked both ways and decided to cross the intersection when, out of the blue, something hit my car. All of a sudden, I could hear the airbag came out, and my car was on the far left side of the street. I could have crossed this intersection in less than 10 seconds, thank God that nobody was hurt, but only the car which I believe had gotten damaged. My point here is that whatever you imagine will come to pass, as the laws of the universe don't deviate the works ideally with the nature of our thought, regardless of whether the thought is positive or negative. To create it, one must use the greatest weapon in the world; it's the imagination. It's a known fact that we can create anything that we imagine; whatever we see around us is the result of someone's thoughts. As a kid, we use our imaginations almost all the time, and when we reach school, our teachers and professors will teach us to conform to what society will accept.

All we need to do is to bring that hidden treasure to the surface and make the whole world benefit from it. To put your imagination to work, you must first become an expert and develop it. Here are some scientific facts, which describe that there are three steps that one must use to create fantasy, theory, and facts. Let's go back in the turn of the century when Edison was building the incandescent light bulb. He had a clear idea in his head on what he needed to develop; he had a theory, and all that was required was to turn it into reality. Anything we see around us once originated in the mind.

If you ask people what they really want, they will look into what they can do. People are accustomed of going into the unseen and discover nature's secret, and how it can be brought to benefit everyone. They leave a mark on this world that gives an idea of who they are. Moreover, in other cases, the majority of people tend not to aim quite high. They try to profit from their incomes to live a lifestyle that they prefer. In other cases, people tend to prefer a justification for their position. They prefer to stay in the zone that they are in. For instance, they would say that they prefer living in a smaller house, driving an old car, etc. They don't aim high, but instead, stay within the bounds.

The reality is that they believe they are unable to receive what they need. As an old saying goes;

"Hate what you can't get." Nevertheless, you cannot attract what you hate.

What is crucial is that you know when you're going the wrong way as opposed to the right way. All the scientific achievements that you see were once unknown; for example, computers, medicine, and so on. The key is that you hold your goal in mind, and everything else will fall into place. If you don't believe this, then there are a large number of billionaires today, you can check their biographies and struggles to see how they reached here today.

To get there, you must begin by using a piece of paper, rather than a device, to write everything that you want. Try not to think about it first, just write down, *"I want..."* and end the sentence with your most profound desires. Go through this exercise and put as much into it as you can. This experiment has proven that around 99.9% of people who write their goals are able to achieve them. This is usually because writing them creates millions of neural pathways to your brain, making you remember it much better. As we mentioned before, we all think on a frequency.

The Bible says,

"As you sow so shall you reap."

And what the law of attraction says is,

"Whatever vibration that you put out, that same vibration is drawn to you like a magnet."

Also, remember that what you're seeking will make its way to you eventually. When you keep your desires alive, it's just a matter of time that you will experience them in your physical world. But first, you must keep the facts clear in your mind and believe in them. However, here is the kicker; most people don't know how to put out the right frequency. They think they are thinking about what they want, but the truth is they are thinking about the lack of it. This means they end up confusing the power and attracting more loss toward them. Remember, the power within tends to multiply everything that you deposit in it. So when you feel like you lack something and continue to think about it, it will increase over time. Your feelings are an essential tool. The feelings are the master tools of creation.

We generally do everything that we do because of the way we feel. This is one of the reasons why professional seminar attendees go to such conferences for years and never get anything accomplished. They are often told to dream bigger, and they go through years of dreaming, but since there's a lack of it coming true, they get frustrated. What you need is the burning desire to succeed.

This is true, and it was, in fact, published in '*the law of success in sixteen lessons*' by Napoleon Hill. At the turn of the century, he was taught by the wealthiest man in the world, and he wrote the law of achievement. His writings changed the lives of many people, including most of today's authors. Hill's materials are what inspired me to write this book. It changed my whole life. That book taught me that to get what you want, you must first research and immerse yourself completely into it. You must define what you want, have faith in your ability to do it, and persist until you have accomplished your goal. You cannot receive that burning desire unless and until you don't turn it into your whole life's mission. Before we can take a step further, I must clarify some facts. Everything in the universe vibrates and meets a different frequency which includes us. The brain is the transmitter and receiver of thought vibration or frequency.

The brain is also an electronic switching station, and the mind is an activity. Most people, when they are asked about their mind, they automatically think of the brain. So here is the question; how can you get what you want? Well, the first goal will be the major indicator, and that is, you must feel good now.

You may consider this goal all the time because, when you feel good, you will never send negative vibrations. Every time you think, you're sending out a vibration. If you think about something for too long, then the duration of the thought will draw toward you like a magnet. Your biggest goal now is to feel good and continue on this path.

To get whatever you want, you must define it first. This definition is up to you and determines whether you want it to be specific or general. The law of attraction will make your dreams come true. When defining what you want by explicitly saying it, it becomes a desire. The good feelings that you get ensure how sure you are about what you need. Negative feelings portray doubts, which is why it's vital to continue a positive attitude and assertive feelings. The primary objective now should be to feel good regardless of your situations and what you're going through. Every day you must monitor how you feel; you have to feel good all day; sing, laugh, and dance.

A friend of mine asked me a question once, *"What about the people who do not know about the law of attraction and yet achieve tremendous success?"* Well, the answer is that the law of attraction works in everyone's life, whether they know about it or not. Because you cannot stop yourself from vibrating energy, hence anytime you think, you tend to transmit vibration. So whatever you put out, by law, it comes back. The biggest challenge is that you have to take that complete responsibility and be the Capitan on the boat. If you don't, you will be part of the crew and be guided by circumstances.

The truth is that whatever you have in your life right now is what you saw in the past. Accordingly, whatever you have now is the result, and the result always tells the truth. If you don't like your result, then you can choose to change the way you think, which is quite significant. The biggest problem with most people is that when they decide to transmit the vibration of what they want, in reality, they are putting the vibration of what they don't have. So the vibration is, *"I don't have…"*

It's essential to create more of what you need. Belief in the undue reality of your thoughts coming true should bring about happiness. You should live every day like its Friday or even payday! When you get to that level of conviction, then you will get everything you desire.

As Napoleon Hill said,

"Whatever the mind of man can conceive and believe, it can achieve."

Let's put it this way; what you want, you will get. What you don't want, you can also get that too; in case you don't send out the right vibrations. There are only four things in the universe; space, time, energy, and matter. However, there's also the fifth, without which nothing could have ever existed; it's infinite intelligence. Remember, it's quite different when you expect something to be on its way, as opposed to when you fear something to be on its way. I had a friend who had a similar event. He was a cab driver in NYC for almost seven years, but before renewing his license, had to have no more than eleven points in the

DMV license to get the approval for the renewal. In his case, he had 39 active points.

He was scared of losing his license, and I told him that he had to imagine that he already had his license. He got happy and submitted the application. A couple of weeks later, I received a call from him saying that he had a miracle. He told me about how he received his renewed license in the mail. It truly works in surprising ways; there's nothing complicated about it, *"as within so without."*

Chapter 4
Change the Way You Think

I believe that thinking shouldn't merely be an act but rather a subject taught in school. This is primarily a necessity after looking at the number of people who confuse everyday activities with the act of thinking. However, upon taking a closer look at people's actions and behaviors, you can easily see how much they lack the ability to think. The mere concept of thought should be a subject that is taught in classes, much like mathematics or learning to play the piano. To become an accurate thinker, you have to start developing tools, much like those that we have described in the previous chapter.

As a matter of fact, all the teachers and philosophers mutually agree on this point. However, they have virtually held many disagreements to certain concepts, such as how you and I can become what we think. Now comes the question; what are you thinking? If you really want to know the answer, then you have to start looking at the result of the question; *"Are you happy with what you have?"* If your answer is negative, then you can change it similar to how you subconsciously made your previous answer.

Now that you're much more aware of the mechanics, you can still apply this information consciously through some effort. This way, you can easily develop a new habit and form a slight imbalance for your betterment. This imbalance sets aside the negative ball of energy that has built up throughout your life. In order to bring about the change, you need to bring about the imbalance by changing the way you think and believe. This way, you can enjoy a 100% difference in your life. You cannot continue to think like you always thought nor continue to believe like you always believed. You must expand your mind and think beyond the ordinary people to get what you want.

As an observer, you have to keep a close look at the people around you; listen to what they say when they talk about lack and limitations. *"Why does this work for me?"* *"Oh, I hate this!"* *"Life sucks."* *"Everything is already accomplished."* *"Dreaming is for losers."* *"The system is controlling us…"* All of these are simply excuses, and it's crucial to know that there is way out. The mind creates these excuses, and they are the vibrations that occur 24/7. However, here is the bad news; the people who own these thoughts are subconsciously great at negative thinking – establishing the *"whys"* of things not working out.

They are the genies of negativity and thus, *'as you sow, so shall you reap.'* These are the people who are the least aware of their life. So much so that their purpose of existence becomes unknown. It's essential to realize that thoughts are a gift from the Creator and to understand that, you need to ask and learn every day continually. When I decided to search for the meaning of my life, I knew I had to change my thoughts. Every goal is set and achieved by the power of the mind. It's mainly conceived by utilizing 99.9% of your thinking ability.

This means that if your thought is correct, then you can transmit the right vibration into the universe. Everything that we see today, along with every advancement, is the thought that people learned to transmit to nature. These thoughts turn into ideas, which then build into a physical reality that ends up benefitting the society we live in. Now, the challenge is that, if you have an idea, then are you willing to explore the gold mine that is within you and bless the world with it? Thoughts are often intangible forces, which are transmitted into never-ending ideas. Stated in another way, ideas live forever, as you think, feel, and believe, so are you.

Every move that you make is your thought; when you decide to go to work, you have to think before leaving. Similarly, when you travel, you have to plan, probably even book a flight, make a reservation, and plan the duration of your vacation, etc. All of this planning takes place in your mind and requires the right thought process to succeed. We can create what we think about. I remember how a couple of years ago, I used to be a cab driver in NYC, as I have shared before. At one point, I had a strange feeling about meeting DMX, my favorite rapper. Subconsciously, I had already thought about meeting him, but I didn't quite understand it.

However, I was wondering whether or not I was serious and whether or not I would actually meet him. Suddenly, it just so happened that one sunny afternoon, I picked up two guys from the West 34th Street, and 10th Ave in Manhattan heading toward Harlem. Harlem is precisely 234 w 125 street. As soon as they entered the cab, they immediately requested if I could quickly take the Westside Highways. Obviously, I obliged, and when we were riding for a couple of minutes on the highway, I took the 125th Street exit, and as we were approaching the traffic signal, I turned toward the right when my passenger gently asked if I could give them two minutes to say hi to a person.

I had no issues, but I was curious to know who the person was, and the guy, to my utter astonishment, replied DMX. I was surprised, to say the least; they mentioned how he was a friend of theirs, and I asked if I could take a few pictures with him. My hands literally shook; I was so excited! Now I realize that it was the law; quite similar to the law of cause and effect, or the law of gravity, or any other laws that have existed in the universe.

Acknowledging the law is one of the wisest things that an individual can do while ignoring it can bring about lack, poverty, limitations, and disaster. You may have thought about it too. It just so happened years ago that one of my dad's friend's son hung himself. My dad heard the story, who later broke the news to us over dinner one evening. The story essentially went like this; my dad's friend had two sons; Ali, the oldest, and Oumarou, the youngest.

Their father recalled to my dad that, as a child, the chores overburdened Ali, and he ended up cleaning the house, cutting woods, and going for groceries. Oumarou, however, got a much more comfortable life as the younger son. While Ali's father had his best interest at heart, Ali's thought process was entirely different. He thought that, rather than training, it was a constant punishment, and the only way to get out of it was by hanging himself. His father held a different view because he felt that, since Ali was the eldest, he would learn responsibility the way his father taught him. Ali's father only tried to walk in his own father's footsteps, but he could not communicate his thoughts to align with his son's. It's important to control our thoughts, so we can control our future. There was another story that had shown up on the news and eventually went viral. It related the story of how a New York cabby from Bayside Queens ended up hanging himself with a belt on November 5th. According to the medical examiner office in NYC, there was no suicide note.

His friend mentioned how the cabby had recently received a taxi medallion the year prior, was $500,000 in debt from a deal and was struggling to stay afloat. Sadly, to get away from the troubles of this life, he decided to take his life. Later, it was reported that over the past few years, around eight cabbies had taken their lives. One of the main reasons is that they fail to realize that when a bad thing happens, it's never really as bad as they thought. On this, nobody said it better than Napoleon Hill,

"Every failure brings with him a seed of equal, or greater benefit."

The law of Polarity as well as states that, for anything to take place, there must be a positive or negative start to it. The price of ignorance can only be death. Here, death doesn't necessarily mean the end of life, but instead, it means that you might end up facing damages sooner or later. I have quite a rich uncle, and a couple of years ago, I was never able to have a proper conversation with him. I could only manage to say *"hello,"* and nothing more. Recently, when I traveled back to Chad, I asked him about his secret to success. With a smile, he simply replied that when he was younger, he used to have an obsession with becoming wealthy.

Even when he didn't have a plan, he still kept talking about how he would be rich someday, and how his world will completely transform. He used to imagine clearly how his life would be clearly. What he did was that he basically put his vibration of what he wanted, and how good it felt. In the end, he finally achieved them. I remember how, when I was 15, I would often go to his house for television and play video games. He had many businesses and eventually had five houses and three cars. As the story continues, after he received everything he wanted, he grew afraid of losing his possessions.

This vibration was utterly different from what it was before he had everything. Now that vibration was focused on loss, and that's precisely what happened. He made a few foolish decisions and ended up losing everything that he had. This is one of the main reasons why people tend to lose their hard work and end up wondering why they did. When they don't have a lot of things, their vibrations are aligned accordingly. They think about their success, feel good about it, and finally, when they've received it, their desire to save it ends up destroying it.

Hill said that the turning point of those who succeeded in life usually comes from a moment of trouble or loss, which one tends to introduce to their real self. However, most of the people, when a difficulty hits them, tend to automatically feel bad or become desperate, instead of focusing on looking for their success. Just remember that whatever is your deepest desire, you will receive. It's not a mere game, but rather, it's a law of the universe. About this, Henry Ford mentioned,

"If you believe that you can or that you can't, either way, you're belief will make it so."

It's essential to understand that your belief is what determines your success; this is simply because it sends out the right vibration, which allows the law to come toward you. If you believe that being successful is mainly your mind's play, then you'll have a 99.9% chance of success. However, if you're working eighty hours weekly and enjoy the work, but it's not a necessity in your path to success, then guess what? That's what you'll get.

After all, your power lies in your ability to think; and we become what we think about most of the time. This is the secret to making everything in your life go according to your plan. Regardless of the work that you put out, what you need to do is align your thinking and your feelings with speculating about the success and the money you want, which is either done consciously or subconsciously. This proves that the majority of what you want is in mind.

Most of the time, people believe that success defines individuals who have a lot of money. However, success is directly proportional to your service, and to be successful, you need to apply the law of compensation by rendering excellent service before you can receive. Success is a habit which is the same as failure. You can genuinely understand success by looking at its spelling in-depth:

S - Sense of direction, U - understanding, C - Courage, C - Compassion, E - Esteem, S - Self-acceptance, S - Self-confidence.

Similarly, you can work out the depth of failure as well:

F - Frustration, A - Aggression, I - Insecurity, L - Loneliness, U - Uncertainty, R - Resentment, E - Emptiness.

Chapter 5
You Must Make a Decision

Imagine being in a position where you notice how your life is turning into a definition of destruction. You feel like everything good that you once had in your life is now slowly moving away from you. However, you did everything that was mentioned in the book, so what was missing? Well, as mentioned, while you might be thinking about the success that you need, what you might have missed out is the clarity of your thoughts. Mostly, what happens in such cases is that you have too many things that you feel are crucial.

Of course, not everything is essential. In this case, your vibrations tend to merge. Ernst Chlandi, a German physicist, studied vibrations, and his work inspired Jenny from Zurich to study the patterns of energy. Looking at the patterns of crystals and fluid, it proved, once again, that your thoughts are part of a much higher energy pattern. The vibrations of your thoughts reflect where you will go in life and just how far you will reach. Considering that, let's take a look at why you often find yourself unable to reach positions where you find success.

To understand this, you can carry out an experiment yourself. Take a pool of water and try creating various vibrations by putting in different objects. You will notice the uncoordinated movement and how, at one point, they tend to merge together. Keeping in mind that your thoughts work the same way. It is usually the beginning of where things go wrong. If I start thinking, *"I want chocolate ice cream,"* and immediately start changing my decision on the flavor, I might end up either not receiving any ice cream, or something that I never really wanted in the first place.

The power of decision has the ability to make or break the pattern that you create for yourself. Ideally, it's essential to keep this in mind; your thoughts will always determine where you reach. As Napoleon Hill once said,

"Our only limitations are those we set up in our own minds."

What this means is that you determine your reality. If you think you have obstacles that you would not be able to overcome, chances are that you will continue to remain in the situation you began with. However, what would happen if you believe that you don't have obstacles, and yet you cannot achieve your potential? In this case, you need to set your thoughts right. What this means is that merely holding a belief wouldn't be enough, you need to set goals one step at a time. Evaluate your goals and decide on what is more critical accordingly. Push yourself to set aside the goals which do not hold as much importance to you, and focus on the ones that would really make a difference. In this case, you need to set time aside to target your thoughts. Organize the pattern of your achievements and decide on your next step.

Minute achievements are often considered as the first step to reaching a significant result. However, what happens, in this case, is that they build up your thoughts to align with receiving what you need in a small amount of time. Always keep in mind that persistence is the key. If you receive those minor achievements in a short timeframe, it doesn't mean that bigger things aren't coming your way, it means that you need to truly believe in them to understand that they too will reach you in due time.

Essentially, as mentioned before, holding out on a large number of desires can also affect your belief in what you want. Making a decision requires confidence in your own ability to achieve. The more confidence you have in your desires, the more chances you have in having them attracted to you. The laws of the universe might seem confusing. However, they teach you one thing, and one thing only; desire. Holding out on many things together means that you don't have enough confidence in yourself to achieve them. Dividing your faith on each desire can affect your chances of receiving them. Instead of being a positive sign, indecision becomes a negative emotion. I'm not saying that it's not possible to not receive everything that you desire, what I'm saying is to charge your energy and vibrations into believing in what is truly significant for you.

Instead of becoming an idea of self-confidence, your decision power also becomes a concept of self-discovery. You start to understand who you indeed are and what you truly need in life. Through the power of decision, you can charge your vibrations to receive the truly important aspects, rather than just the minor and insignificant things, which you might not benefit from in the long run. Can you make a decision? I ask this because it's not something that is easy for many people. The people who can reach the top and actually get somewhere in life are the ones who are able to make a decision quite fast and not change their mind later.

On the other hand, there are indecisive people who are the ones with difficulties in making a decision and sticking to it. Why people tend to slack around is quite simple. Here's an example; let's say that you decided to go to the airport, but you aren't familiar with the city. You start driving, and every four miles, you turn around and go the other direction. You can either continue on this route or keep doing the same thing every four miles. This means that the lack of direction, or a constructed and researched plan can result in indecisiveness.

Drifting emptily throughout your whole life can be quite consequential. You have to make a decision and discover your purpose. This is the only thing that could help you, but what's really important is that you act upon the discovery and send the relative vibration into the universe. Once you consistently send it out, it will grow into a positive result. Many people use this word by saying, 'I had to go to the gym today, but I changed my mind.' In this case, it's essential to pay attention to where your mind is.

The majority of the people have no control over their minds and like they believe that they do. I had a friend whose uncle moved to the U.S. in the 80s. His first job in America was as a dishwasher, and he worked for almost a year. He then moved on to driving a cab for fifteen years until he had enough. He was adamant on success and wanted to make use of his CDL. Since then, he spent 35 years driving a trailer, but sadly, still remains broke and poor. Yet, he doesn't change his mind. What I'm asking for is that you pick out the missing ingredient in this story. While you probably didn't know, or maybe even you did, his uncle lacked the power of decision making. My question to you what is the missing ingredient here, you probably know or not, there is only one that is the lack of a simple decision. He never took out the time to learn about himself and his sole reason for living. Now, it was too late for him to make a change, and he stood at one place, wondering where he went wrong.

The worst part was that the long driving hours resulted in damages caused by driving for over fifty years. He had neglected the greatest gift and failed to use it properly. If he had, it could have brought his desires to life. Each of us has this gift, but only a few people can discover it. It's crucial to take notice of this; would you rather be like the uncle who wasted his entire life working without reaping the rewards? Would you not want peace and contentment that comes after the struggle? Would you instead sit in the middle of bad traffic, stressing yourself out? I'm sure that's not what you want.

These days, students are unaware of the field that they want to specialize in, and that's just as bad. When I moved to New Jersey City University, I had a friend with whom I struck up a conversation one time. He asked me what my major was, and I replied saying that I was pursuing finance. A couple of weeks later, he changed his field to finance as well.

Why is this incident relevant? Well, it's because no matter what the choices are, an indecisive person will always fail to make a decision about their future, or even wait to see it manifest. Reports say that there are over seventy-five percent of Americans who don't like their jobs. However, the truth of the matter is that no one forces them to work. It's just the pressure that builds up from the bills that makes them go out and make a living. While people might show that they are happy, that is just an empty statement.

However, the condition of the heart is a different matter. Doubt, anger, frustration, and limitations are what stop it from making a decision about quitting their job and finding something that they love to do. Usually, this something else makes you enjoy your work and do it perfectly. If, however, you don't like what you do, then make sure that you don't complain and set a goal that you must follow at any cost. Your life would be very different if you put your plan into action instead. This will make your life so much easier. One of the main reasons that people tend to suffer is because of the lack of decisions, and students believe that it's their degree that will bring their success. However, that is not true. School might teach you valuable knowledge, but it doesn't give you the life lessons you genuinely need, such as the art of decision making. The first thing that students are given is debt, especially in this country. Secondly, some of the biggest companies today wouldn't want to hire a fresh graduate. They need people with at least three to four years of experience.

The odds of this happening are quite slim, and it's difficult for them to adapt and learn the tricks of a work environment because companies usually don't want to waste time training new employees. In this case, a fresh graduate would rather take up the first opportunity they get, which means that they would prefer not applying their learnings from school into their career. This wouldn't benefit their future employer or society at all. This lack of decision on their future movements is what affects them significantly. As I have studied banking and finance, to me, I desired to land a great job after graduation, and this would be specific to banking. Regardless of what the future held, I decided that I would never go for any random job, which has no connection to my line of work. If this decision is made and implemented, then most students would face the success that they crave. One day, my dad told me a story about the richest man in his village. It was no accident that made him so wealthy, it was his determination. When he was twenty, this man left the village because of famine, lack of money, lack of water, and a host of other problems.

He decided that he would move to the capital, but his greatest challenge was that he didn't even have a dime. The distance from the city was about 500 miles, and he told himself that he would head to the bus station the next day and ask any driver to give him a lift. That afternoon, he went to the bus station to get the relevant information. However, he noticed a black plastic bag strewn at the side of the street.

Without any knowledge on what was inside it, he opened it and found about $2000 inside. Since it wasn't his money, he decided to wait for someone to come and claim it, but he waited from 4:30 PM to 8:00 PM, and no one showed up. It was then that he was convinced the money was the answer to his prayers. Until morning, he remained convinced about moving to the city, so he hopped on the bus. After riding about 100 miles, they stopped at a village where, as per tradition, a vendor comes by to sell items. It could be fruits, grains, jewelry, food, and other varieties of item. The guy hops off the bus for some fresh air and, on the opposite side, he saw a gentleman selling smoked fish in a large bag.

He asked for the price, and something told him to buy the wholesale fish and sell it elsewhere. He took it as an epiphany and asked the driver if there was space for his items. Since the price didn't seem too high, and the bus driver had space, the guy bought over 34 bags of fish for a bargain price. He was now on his way to the capital as a businessman. Once they arrived, there was a crisis of smoked fish, and it seemed like the entire city was in need. Buyers lined up and waited for his fish. He sold it at twenty times the original price, and, since then, he has hired a truck to carry the fish. In less than two years, the guy became a millionaire.

If you read the story carefully, you'll understand that the magic ingredient for his success was his decision making power. If he had stayed in the village after finding the money, he wouldn't be able to achieve the success he has today. Real success is measured by the power you hold in decision making and by cutting off the moments where you want to retreat. People facing difficulties in life forget how to stick to what they want. They let their parents make all the necessary decisions. If they end up stacking everything up, the result will always be a disaster. Independence is something that will take you a long way; listening to other people's opinions, or relying on them to make your decision could end up in failure. Everyone will have an opinion about your life, what you need to do is make sure that you stay firm at what your solution is.

The other issue that most people have is regarding procrastination. What is procrastination, you ask? Well, it's when you put off some job or work to a later date. Let's say that you want to quit your job and start a business. Procrastinators would keep delaying it by saying they'll quit next month. Next thing you know, ten years down the road, they're still there working at the same position.

Due to the lack of knowledge on technique, they fail to research and learn and then end up doing the same thing over and over again. This is usually because giving up is much easier than putting in the effort. There is an old saying, *"You can make yourself a donkey or a horse; it's up to you whether you choose failure or success, you can choose knowledge, or stay ignorant. The final decision is yours."* Years ago, Andrew Carnegie scored over thousands of employees, but he found none to be equal or excel over him. The thing they lacked was decision making and the ignorance of thought. They were thinking that getting the work done was the secret to success, but it was rendering service to others, which was the real solution. If you have a good job and income that would be able to fit your lifestyle and get you everything you desired, then there's nothing wrong with what you're doing.

Even if you're not able to afford all the luxuries of life, like a private jet or a mansion, that's ok. What matters is that you can live a decent life with your family, stay within the boundaries, and not have to struggle to make ends meet. If, however, you're simply getting through life and cater to stress through every step of the way, then you're not doing it right.

If you have to make sure that you are simply getting by and by, then it's not called true success. You need to understand that not even your family relies on you as much as you think. You don't need to have everything figured out, you can't just help everyone. In the process, instead of helping them, you might put them at risk. Keep in mind that, to be a successful entrepreneur, you have to pause your limited life and go serve the world with integrity, then you will reap the harvest; it can be no other way. Focusing on rendering valuable service to others must be the first goal. This is going to be the biggest challenge yet, but you cannot hold on to your old life. If you want to move ahead, you have to adapt to the challenges that come your way. While I know that we usually don't plan to fail, our subconscious is continuously thinking about the consequences. While failing may not be the end vision, it is the puzzlement that comes in the process.

Try to correct it and rearrange your attitude to keep moving ahead. A quitter never wins, and a winner never quits. When President Theodore Roosevelt was staying at the Hotel Gilpatrick in Milwaukee, Wisconsin on October 14th, 1912, he was sitting outside the hotel with a 50-page manuscript in hand. He folded it in half and slipped it into the breast pocket of his overcoat.

After he stood up to head out for his campaign speech, he was shot point-blank by someone from the crowd. Luckily, the manuscript's papers stopped the bullet from penetrating into his lung. When you make a decision, there is absolutely no going back from it. Roosevelt had made a prompt decision, and even his meeting with death didn't stop him from giving his speech.

The man who marked the beginning of the end of the Berlin Wall didn't do it by accident. He had already envisioned it in his mind. While most people believed that it was announced by accident, those events already had taken place in the mind. For students who know the mind's law, there is no such thing as coincidences. The beginning of the end of the cold war was actually announced by accident by a man named Gunther Schabowski, on November 9th, 1989. The East German communist office was addressing a news conference when a journalist posed a question about travel restrictions.

He responded that a regulation would be implemented, allowing citizens of the German democratic republic to leave East Germany via any of the border crossings along the Berlin wall. Although the information wasn't supposed to be released until 4 AM the following day, Schabowski's words immediately spurred the wall's collapse. This proves that every event occurs because the laws don't let you deviate. For every cause, there is an effect, even though we don't know the effects. The buying of the Louisiana territory by the American President easily supersedes the thrill of driving RVs across challenging terrain.

Thomas Jefferson took advantage of Napoleon's need for conquering Europe, which led to this sale. Since Napoleon wanted to limit England's influence in America, he obviously needed money to return to the government coffers after the war. This is why Napoleon offered an entire territory, which was worth much more than the $15 million for which it was sold.

This is a great example of how, sometimes it could be pure luck, and other times, it's the power of decision that grants success. When chasing your dream, you must make a prompt decision and stick with it, so others understand your plan. Then you must be persistent and remember that failures cannot be coaxed with persistence alone.

YASSINE O OUMAR

Chapter 6
Believe and Achieve

Now that we understand the universe and its laws, let's look into one of the most significant struggles that people often face; belief. While it's easier said than done, holding out belief can be quite challenging. To be a person of belief, you must first forgive yourself and then move on to forgiving others. Here, the belief required is more related to the belief in your ability to achieve.

Often, people say that faith can move mountains, but that's not actually true. Faith is actually an understanding of your ability. If you think that you have the power to do so, then you will. The only mystery that's left of this concept is neglect. Faith is something that's available to every humble person the same way as to the influential people, but keep in mind that without faith, any work is entirely useless.

When I was in the process of building my mobile application months ago, I decided to tell my friend about it. I was looking for a developer, but I couldn't find one that suited my budget. It was then that I asked myself if the application was something I really wanted. It was a way to re-affirm what I wanted and how I would do it if I was serious. In conclusion, I kept aside my budget and put my main focus on what I had in mind. When talking to my friend about it, he asked me how much it would cost. I replied with a smile and tenacious thousands of dollars. This left him shook as he exclaimed how serious I was and where I would get that kind of funding. I reassured him and told him that when it's time, the money will automatically come.

My friend was convinced that I was insane and that I should look at the situation more thoroughly. I told him that I had learned a long time ago that when you have made a decision and have the right attitude, the facts don't count. Fast forwarding to a couple of months down the road; upon the project's approval, I send them the payment upfront, so they could kickstart it.

Developers typically work by setting milestones. This is the only thing that made me believe that when you decide to do something, you have to just do it and don't think about the 'how' factor. It is an irrelevant factor; when the development of the app began, it was based on ideas submitted to them, which were outlined clearly. However, the end result was completely different from what was expected. What I received at the end was a phenomenon, which was ten times more than what I had expected before the development began. My friend refused to read a book, regardless of how much I persisted. In the end, he continued to move in the wrong path. Because he refused to expand his mind and learn, when I informed him of my development progress, he was shocked and refused to believe it.

I told him that he didn't really have to believe me since it wasn't his dream, but mine. All I know is that I didn't need a reason, all I knew was that I was getting there, and I would stop at nothing to get what I want. This is one of the biggest reasons why, as per my belief, most people failed to achieve their goal. They always have disbelief in heart and then focus on *"how."* It's crucial to note that the *"how"* society usually talks about is much different.

They refer to it in a positive light. That means; they relate to the skill, technic, method, and plan in order to move to the opposite side of the scale and bypass the how. That's why people cannot see how, by creating alibis, they keep them in a position of never achieving anything. It's this scripture that refers to faith as a substance of what you hope for. It's the evidence of the unseen. Thus, my friend told me to look at the facts instead, and I had ignored him. I, instead, followed my plan and eventually reached my goal. After all, his ignorance was what will lead him never to see what is beyond his current situation. The important thing to succeed is to have belief and know what it is to believe. It's a picture in your mind that your senses and the word of reason denies. An accepted thought executes itself automatically through the subconscious mind. After being in the country for years, I decided to pay a visit to my family back home. However, before going home, I envisioned my own mental movie, where I was the director. In the movie, I automatically imagined a horror movie where I could see loss and a very tough time coming ahead. During that time, I saw that I didn't read, and the worst part was, I wasn't aware of my mind's law.

It was in those days that I bought a brand new Ford Fusion and decided to send it before landing in my home country. Since I have never sent a car before, I subconsciously knew that I was incompetent, and so, I decided to take help from a friend of mine, Usman Kara, who frequently sends cars. We scheduled a day and then went to the Bayonne port of New Jersey. There, we talked to the guy who worked in the shipping line and finalized the paperwork. Basically, you need a cosigner who will unload the car from the boat on the final destination, which was Chad in my case. The vehicle has to go through the transit port of Benin, and everything would be done. It's quite complicated, and I'm sure I wouldn't have been able to do it without my friend. A week after visiting the dock, I received a call from a guy who also used to be a driver. He currently owns a dealership, and I was genuinely impressed. He called to inform me how he worked with my older brother his whole life and that I should heed his warning about the car that I sent back home.

This caught my attention. He asked me to go back to the shipping line and have them change the car transit paperwork. It had to be changed to his name so that he could send someone to check the car upon arrival. Usually, they steal new tires and sell them back to you. I understood what he was saying, and so I immediately ran back to the shipping line and had the name changed right then.

I expected the car to reach Chad before I got there, but a month later, there was still no sign of it. After two months, I lost patience and found out that the car hadn't left the customs yet. Finally, I was told that the car's paperwork received by the customs in Benin clearly stated that the final destination is Benin. This meant that the custom's paperwork had to be done, and it's cost turned out to be the market price of the car.

I decided then that I should let it go. However, I suddenly had an epiphany to head off to Benin and check what the blockage was. I went through the desert and finally reached Benin. Finding the car seemed impossible, but something kept telling me that I was already there. I had a feeling telling me that if I believed in something, I could definitely do it. I ran to various offices in hopes of getting my car out. However, all I heard from them was that it was quite difficult and impossible to do anything in this situation.

I suddenly received a call from a guy who asked me if I needed help with my situation. Of course, I did, and I affirmed it to the guy on call as well. He told me to go and meet him at a rendezvous point. I absolutely couldn't believe what I was hearing; he said that he could get the car out in less than twenty-four hours. I couldn't thank him enough for all his help, and it indeed affirmed my belief that if you have a feeling or epiphany, then you must follow it.

Everyone striving success needs to follow his or her feeling and move from the thought stage into the feeling stage. I had to borrow quite a lot of money from my older brother to get the car to its final place, and I knew I had to pay him back. Once I reached home, I had a difficult time finding a buyer, and the prices being offered were too low and significantly less than the cost of the car. I left it in charge of my brother because I owed him a lot of money, and in the end, the car was parked in the dealer parking lot officially for sale. I left Chad and headed back to the U.S., but before leaving, I had many violation tickets and assigned them to my lawyer. My stay in Chad was supposed to be for one month and ended up being five months instead. In all those months, all I did was stay at home and wait for the ticket prices to decrease.

My attorney tried reaching me so many times, but it went straight to voicemail. When I reached the U.S., I immediately contacted my lawyer, who told me that my license had been revoked. This was one of the toughest times that I went through, and it simply kept on getting worse. However, the only thing that kept me going was my attitude to everything going on.

Regardless of everything negative in my life, I still felt good. Every day, I kept reassuring and telling myself that everything was going to be okay. I may not have any assurance of how I would get through this situation, I still had my faith. I knew in my heart that everything was going to be just fine. One night, as I sat in bed and scrolled through YouTube, I came across a video which was shot in the 60s, I believe. The video was titled, *'Do you know who you are?"* That's what intrigued me. Even though I usually scroll past such videos, this one, in particular, kept pulling me toward it. I figured that I might as well just watch it. It turned out to be an interview of a philosopher, Bob Proctor. The video captivated me so much that I watched it entirely until the end.

During the interview, he mentioned another book by Napoleon Hill, 'Think and grow rich.' It hyped me up so much that I immediately went to Amazon and purchased the book. I read the book dozens of times and combined its teachings with that of Mr. Proctor's materials. The two of them became my Masters, guiding me to the success I have today.

I'm quite sure that I wasn't attracted to this video by accident; it was a definite answer to my prayers. It made me love myself and have an intense gratification for my inner being. The works of Mr. Proctor and Mr. Hill helped me discover a lot about myself and gained the willingness to learn. Thinking back to everything that I went through, it was Napoleon Hill's book that meant the world to me.

It is honestly acknowledged as the greatest seed that I received after all the difficulties I had to face. I wasn't defeated mentally, and I was starting to look at myself as a winner already. I truly believe that a moment of crisis is the turning point for winners, it's all about what you choose to do with it. Years ago, a friend of mine was telling me a story about their neighbor's dog. Without a dog, they would be robbed practically every night and decided that it was time to get a guard dog.

This pet patrolled the yard every night, and in the morning, it was kept caged up. Since they bought a dog, they weren't robbed once. However, the dog, once released at night, would join another pack and return in the morning. One night, the dog fell into a deep hole of about two thousand feet, and the next morning, the owner couldn't find him. The dog was missing for two whole days, and they were quite worried.

The hole was next to a soccer field, and on the third day, when the kids were playing around, the ball fell into the hole as well. That was when they found the dog and immediately moved to action. They brought a basket and slowly pushed it into the hole until it reached the ground. The dog was able to reach it, jump in, but when they pulled up, he would jump out again. This lasted for five days, and finally, he perished. What does this story have to do with you? Well, it shows that when people are in bad situations, they will become hopeless, like the dog was. Instead, they need to rearrange their attitude and look for seeds of greatness. This is one of the biggest reasons why, when people are broke, they tend to stay that way for the rest of their lives; they lack faith. The Bible said,

"Everything that he believes is possible for him."

Williams James said, at the turn of the century,

"Believe, and your belief will make the fact."

If you opt for a job, regardless of what it is, you need to make sure you keep your savings. If you keep repeatedly spending for about fifty or sixty years and then lose your job, you might as well just end up homeless. It's essential to remember that the saved amount is not as significant as the habit of saving. Statistics show that most people pass away without fulfilling their dreams.

They fail to discover themselves and end up using the mind's law against them. It is also often in fear of something wrong happening to their children. Most people believe that they can't amount to anything and that they can't build their business because of the lack of resources. The major problem that people usually focus on is resources, and most importantly, the facts. If you focus on the fact, then there's an excellent chance that you might end up being broke for a long time. Take note of anyone who achieved greatness. In most or all of such cases, people didn't know much about how to receive it. What they did know, however, is that they had a dream, and they wanted to achieve it at all costs. Some people might have a dream to become a billionaire at the age of fifteen, while others at twenty-three or thirty, etc.

However, they might fail to achieve it because of the lack of confidence in their abilities. Let me tell you a little secret; sometimes, you need to bypass logic and understand your feelings. If you have an interest in something, then none of the facts would work, and your feelings would be in total control of it. The law of attraction would make it work.

Therefore, your magic ingredient to success is your feeling and your confidence. You must follow the two, regardless of the circumstances, so you can easily make sure you get the required result. The secret to believing in anything is the power of the repetition of information. It's been said that even if you lie, repeating the statement constantly will make you believe it.

This belief is the realization that it's not long before the physical manifestation occurs as events, situations, and circumstances. I have a close friend, Onyema Alhadj, who had applied for a student visa for more than six times. I failed to understand his mind back then, and what his experience was inside of him. However, I can still see the desire in his eyes. As I mentioned before; you can lie about your own statement, you'll eventually start believing it. Every time my friend talked about the U.S., his eyes lit up with excitement. However, since he tried and failed so many times, all of the evidence seemed to be opposing it.

However, he finally got a job at a refinery, got married, and was blessed with beautiful children. Since I left him and moved to New York, we lost contact with each other. However, I later received a call from him saying that he would like to come to the U.S. for a two-month-training session, and he would be coming to New York, right where I was staying. He completed his paperwork; however, his position didn't guarantee a visa. He was scared, but I asked him if he would believe my secret. He was adamant on finding a way, so he agreed. I asked him how he would feel if I told him he received the visa right now.

He told me that he would be exhilarated. I told him that the secret is to feel exactly like you would if your visa was already here; not when it's in the process, but when you're holding it in your hands. It's essential to also give thanks for the approval in advance and feel the conviction of imagining whatever you want and feeling exactly like you would if it was yours. On the day of the interview, he went in by keeping my thoughts in mind and believing that these were just non-issues.

Usually, when they reject you, they send back all the documents immediately. However, when his interview was done, they kept his documents for review, and they would then make a decision on whether or not it's approved. He called me up right then and kept on thanking me for letting him in on the secret. This was the first time that he was able to turn his defeat into victory. There were many ways that this event could have played out; he could have not listened to my advice, pushed me away, or simply hadn't listened to me. However, he stood firm and took matters into his own hands, just as I had suggested.

This world has two types of struggling people; those who were told but never took action, and those who did absolutely nothing. Some people tend to send conscious and subconscious thought vibration to the universe, but when there's an unexpected opportunity or incident, they don't take action. There was a story that was mentioned in a seminar of my favorite mentor. This was about the minister of the Louisiana Church, and how the flood was coming. During this time, the entire city was evacuated. When the time for evacuation came, he mentioned that he would not go and be part of the ships; he was adamant that God would take care of him.

Thus, once the second boat came by, he decided to stay back, even though everyone was talking about how he would die here. The water was rising, and the preacher stood on the roof of a chapel, committed to his decision. A helicopter came by, and he refused to go again. When the water continued to rise, he was swept away and drowned. However, once he reached Heaven, he was furious and asked that he believed in God and the Bible, and yet he wasn't saved. St. Peter replied, saying that he was an idiot. Three boats and a helicopter were sent to him, but he refused to take action.

This shows the importance of action; that while having faith is vital, it's equally important to take action as well. The action that you take today will shape your life and determine your future. At the age of twenty-three, Sir Isaac Newton watched an apple fall from a tree in his mother's orchard. The apple never really hit him on the head, but it did provide support for his gravitational theory. In 1665, Sir Newton had formulated the three laws of motion. One of them is *"For every action is an equal, but opposite reaction,"* and for this, his explanation often applied to physical objects and forces.

"As you sow, so shall you reap" is relatively the same thing. Every law is quite similar, and we never pay attention to them. Nothing is accidental.

The only issue with these things is that of ignorance, which can result in rage, unhappiness, poverty, and limitations. The best example is that of listening to the wrong or bad music. Scientists are not quite able to explain frequency and how they can pass through brick, steel, trees, and other solid objects. Imagine turning on the radio and suddenly hearing music all around. This is simply because of frequency and energy transfer.

"Everything is energy and that's all there is to it. Match the frequency of the reality you want and cannot help but get that reality; there can be no other way. This is not philosophy. This is physics."

Albert Einstein

But how does it work?

Well, it's easy. Knowledge is omnipresent, which means it can be at every place at the same time. Now imagine sending a message to someone in the opposite room. They would be able to receive it instantly. All that's needed is awareness, everything here is simply the concept of allowing yourself to become more aware of using this knowledge and power. This will help you create the life you want. It's only a matter of understanding and then putting it into application.

People end up making $50,000 a year when they could be making a lot more. If you ask them whether or not they want to increase their income, they would reply with a definite answer. However, what they lack is their ability to stay in focus. Again, focusing on the *"how"* is what would affect their ability to earn the amount they need. As mentioned before, this factor is what allows you not to see or imagine what you can receive.

The crucial point is never to focus on it, or else your dream will become worthless. To gain success, you need first to think, act, talk, and feel like a success; day in and day out. Most of the people believe in the idea that *"Seeing is believing;"* however, the most exceptional people believe it even before seeing it.

One of the most prominent examples is when a steel magnate was once asked the secret to success. He replied that it was the ability to put all your eggs into one basket and then keep a watch on that basket, which remains as following one goal. The energy becomes centralized and brings it toward you.

Chapter 7
The Subconscious Mind

The subconscious mind is the storehouse of information. The mind is known to have two spheres of activities.

The conscious mind; It is the mind which is also known to be the thinking mind where the five senses are located. These senses (touch, see, hear, smell, and taste) would collaborate with the external, physical world. The conscious mind is also the educated mind, where intellect is the resident, and its primary purpose is to help you choose, originate, accept, or reject an idea. This is the main focus of every school, where you have the ability to decide on the most critical aspects of your life, or even carry out any planning.

The universal mind; this is also known to be the subjective or the emotional mind. The universal mind takes all the information given to it by the conscious mind or thinking mind, and it doesn't have the ability to reject it.

The beauty of the subconscious mind is that it doesn't know the difference between reality and imagination. Most importantly, the body is the mind's instrument. Before the body carries out any activity, the action must occur in the mind first. Now, one of the most common questions that readers might have is, *"How do we form a habit?"* Well, it's quite easy, really. Let's take driving a car as an example. You need to first go back into your memory and recall what it was like to first drive. To reach the level of perfection of an incredible driver, first you had to undergo repetition. This means that you continued to practice until you became a pro. The knowledge was stored in your subconscious, and you could do it without putting a thought into it. You were finally on a knowledge bank, which was on the subconscious level.

Now let's look at a different perspective; I'm going to talk in terms of my childhood. My parents are from Chad, which means that the only language they speak is Arabic. Once they immigrated to Central African Republic, the language spoken there was Sango. The schools there solely taught in French, since the country was a French colony. However, when we would travel to Chad every now and then, I decided to learn English as well. Thus, I spoke four languages; English, Arabic, Sango, and French.

Growing up, I had the idea that I only knew one language, which was right in its own way. This is because I grew up with the idea that I could only speak one language. The truth is that, even if you learn several languages, your subconscious mind will automatically consider only the language you speak most frequently. The mind will accept everything good or bad, and repetition is the key to building a prominent personality.

When we are born, our sensory aspects of communication are not developed. As a baby, your subconscious mind is wide open, and the five senses aren't as developed yet either, as an old saying declares, give me a child until his age is seven, and I will show you the man. When a baby is surrounded by parents, their influence, and the environment itself will affect the information they receive every day.

This will continue every day, month, and year until the age of five. Now the baby is programmed genetically, this is why he/she tends to look like his parents or relatives. This time, he is programmed environmentally during his early childhood years. If the baby's parents prefer, then they would send him to school; similarly, if they are poor or lack resources, then the baby will face those issues as well.

Many people are programmed since birth and fail to alter this programming throughout their life. Similarly, in most cases, the conscious mind is open to the world and absorbs in the negativity that surrounds them. This is why the majority of the people are affected by the issues that they go through this life while in poverty and fail to use that as an excuse to exercise the mind. To alter the older programming, which has exclusive control over your thinking, you must do this every minute, so you can climb up the ladder of success. If you're always talking about the lack in your life, then that is what you will face.

If you're looking forward to creating the life you always wanted, then you must first move on from what you don't want and listen to your desires. This is because talking about what you don't want will always bring about frustration and delays. Eventually, you will notice that you would reach a level of *not reaching* anywhere in life. The only thing that will surely grow is what you would put your attention to. It's important to remember that the subconscious mind focuses on what the conscious mind hands it. It will then be magnified, thereby allowing you to attract more delay in your mission. All of these delays are significant evidence of the energy that you are vibrating.

The conscious mind is often known to be the jealous mind, which lets go of what you're enthusiastic about, or something that you are scared from. Eventually, it becomes your mission to protect this abundant garden of your mind. It's always crucial to remember that your subconscious mind is like a garden, and your conscious mind is the gardener. Every day, through the power of thought, you seed and water the garden, and those thoughts control the vibrations that you are in.

This means that your feeling is also a vibration. You would not notice a difference unless you move onto the level of feeling. Thus, when you think of something on the conscious mind, you basically emotionalize how those thoughts would go directly into your subconscious mind; this automatically would change the vibration. Your feeling would automatically change accordingly.

The feeling that pushes you to act, leads to an action that would set up an attraction, thereby altering the effect. You need to understand how your conscious and subconscious mind work related to your body. Therefore, this is the magic behind any dominating thoughts, ideas, plans, or purpose which is held in mind. It begins at once to transform itself into physical reality through the most convenient method available. The subconscious mind is the gateway connecting a man's finite mind with infinite intelligence. The subconscious reveals knowledge to those seeking it, and the answer is clearly visible to you, as an intuition, inspiration, symbol, hunches, ideas, feelings, or even through friends. The next step of acting upon them is simply up to you. Many years ago, I had a friend who lived in New York and drove a cab. He was issued three summons by the New York taxi limousine commission officers. One ticket was there because he failed to stop at a stop sign, the other two were for wearing headphones while driving.

He was convinced that his TLC license would be suspended or revoked automatically for finding him guilty. I told him whatever he believes would eventually turn into reality. I explained to him the power of imagination and further encouraged him to believe positive thoughts of his circumstances, events, and situations. This included picturing that his problem was solved, and that he won all the tickets from the court. On his first trial, the judge was there, and soon the TLC representative showed up and informed of an issue in their system. Therefore, they withdrew the first ticket.

On the second trial, the same statement was given by the representative who told the judge that the problem was on-going in their system, and the ticket would be withdrawn. Finally, the last ticket had the same outcome. This time, when heading to court, he ran into a friend of his who was tried for a similar ticket. My friend came out of the court with a dismissed ticket again, and a couple of minutes later, his friend came out being found guilty.

The truth of the matter is, whatever is mentally pictured and believed would soon become a reality. As James Williams said, *"At the turn of the century. Any picture held in the mind backed by faith will come to pass. Our behavior is habitual, and as soon as we pass culture, we are all the same."* How we form our habit is through repetition or through the observation of someone else, who has succeeded in doing something that you consider as your goal.

Through observation, you can emulate their actions and behaviors into your work. The repetition of doing what they have done while working on a different frequency is what produces excellent results. Repetition is known to be the best way to form a new habit; it's similar to how you repeat a lie so many times that you start believing it.

Think back and see how often you have talked to your friends about changing your life. They've laughed at, and with you, and tell you to be satisfied with what you have. If you accepted it, then you're not any different than them. However, if you understand that limitation is only in the mind or what others have set for you, then you know you can achieve wonders. What you fail to understand, if you listen to them, is that dissatisfaction is a creative stage. While you can be happy with what you have, the key is that you shall never be satisfied. How many times have you seen others make a decision to do something different and work on it? The program dictates and attracts that something different would always produce undesirable results.

Nobody can approach the universal mind with fear, the power that can move the world is only available in your subconscious mind. Through the power of the unknown, the subconscious mind will draw to the power of infinite intelligence to transform a desire into reality. Keep in mind that your desire is your prayer. If you know the importance of a prayer's power, then your whole life would turn into a prayer. Neglecting the proper use of the mind would result in several issues regarding your health, relationships, happiness, and your wealth. Anything you want is in your DNA because, whatever you vibrate will come to pass, but the difference would be either negative or positive. The subconscious mind fails to understand the difference between right or wrong, or even between positive or negative. This is usually why a penny or even a million dollars would be accepted through affirmation and will turn into a habit. Your subconscious mind works all the time without any rest. All the activities that automatically occur in your body, like breathing or lung function in your sleep, are done through your subconscious mind. You need to learn how to build a relationship with that portion of your mind and use it to transform your life.

It is through this power that you would be able to accomplish anything in a year or less, especially if you're on a mission to explore this rich garden of your mind. Don't look outside for opportunities since whatever you want is inside of you already. All you lack is awareness, and once you achieve that, you would be able to gain the success you were waiting for. Because your subconscious doesn't know the law of averages, or how to magnify and multiply, and have you live in abundance or poverty.

This way, you can enjoy the friend that you find within yourself and get surrounded by beauty and luxury. Always keep in mind that you have the key to anything you want, and you have the symbol of ultimate wellness for yourself. Belief is the ultimate key. To achieve greatness in your life, you need to be able to make personal sacrifices. Make sure that you keep your past in the past and move on to facing new challenges and growing from the problems you had to face.

From today onwards, you are a whole new person, and it's your mission to have a good heart, and serve as well as love the world around you. Also remember that a man's faith is tested many times, and the key to allowing greatness to come forward from such tasks is to express your true self.

That means, don't allow that test to drag you down, but instead, make sure that you stay true to making everything right. Imagine you're the pilot, and your life is the plane. Let me ask you something, in case of an emergency, would you separate yourself from your passengers, or would you keep a firm hand and try to keep the plane and your passengers in control? It's probably the latter, right? Well, just like you'll maintain your faith then, once your life is in peril, you will react the same way.

"If you can believe, all things are possible to him who believes."

-Mark 9:23

Belief is known to be a thought in your mind, which is accepted by the subconscious mind and denied by your senses and voice of reason. Any thought once accepted by the subconscious mind, it will get automatically executed; just like aforementioned, *"As you believe, so it shall be done."*

"The greatest discovery of my generation is how human beings can alter their life by altering the attitude of their mind."

-Williams James

This is also a scripture from the Bible, which says, *"As a man thinks in his heart, and so is he."* In reality, people are often confused and tend to dig up roots to look for fruits, whereas there are others who simply search for which fruits to pick out.

"Whatever we plant in our subconscious mind and nourish with repetition and emotion will one day become a reality."

-Earl Nightingale

Chapter 8
Know the Laws of the Universe

Now that we've seen how you could achieve success, it's time we properly discussed the laws of the universe that you genuinely need to pay attention to. Here are the most important universal laws for your knowledge:

Law of Mentalism/Attraction

When trying to understand the secret principles that control your life patterns, it's essential to begin your journey by looking at the most fundamental principle. This is something that resides within you and can be controlled by you alone. The law of mentalism states that your reality is within your mind; it is basically your perception.

We live in the Divine mind, and so everything we perceive as reality is the essence of mentalism. If you want to achieve true success, you need to align your thoughts according to what you want your reality to be. According to the law of mentalism, you can achieve success through the aspects of reality you keep your focus on. Here's an example that you might find interesting.

It wasn't too long ago when I was preparing for my college exams. During those times, my friends and I went through a car crash, which was quite a traumatic experience for all of us. In essence, it affected our perspective, and while none of us sustained any serious injuries, we were all equally shaken from the experience. Fast forward to a couple of months later; while we all had recovered, I started to face some personal problems as well. I had absolutely no hope of passing the exams.

I was in a place where I had to figure myself out before facing any more issues, and that's when I got the intel on *"The law of mentalism."* It was quite an eye-opener when I realized that it was true, I was basing my life on focusing on the negative of reality. It was time for a change, and for that, I had to begin with my mind. My journey started when I started to perceive the positive and focus on the things that actually mattered.

It was a massive change for me, as things started to unfold quite well. In those times, I also noticed that my concentration on the more important part of my life – my studies – increased as well. The only true test to show whether or not this theory worked were my results. I spent the days after the exam visualizing excellent grades, and guess what happened? I passed! While my friends, who were more caught up on their trauma, didn't pass quite as expected, they were quite surprised at my grade. I let them in on my secret, and after research, they decided to live according to this law as well. Needless to say, it worked for them too!"

What we don't realize is that our reality is nothing but what our mind's make it. It's vital to know that success can be defined by the subconscious mind, which is fed by the conscious mind. Once you have that taken care of, you'll be able to achieve anything.

Law of Gender

The law of gender is quite simple, it talks about creating a balance within our bodies, which are determined by the genders within us. While some people may believe that gender only exists in plants and animals, it's necessary to understand that everything has masculine and feminine properties, and understanding the two is what can bring about a significant difference in our lives; like the Yin and Yang. Every person has certain aspects in their personality, which determines who they are; what they don't realize is that gender isn't just about the physical plain. Everything has two qualities:

The feminine aspects are those that determine the creative, subconscious mind, empathic, compassionate, collaborative, and intuitive right-brained thinking.

The masculine aspects are those that determine the power of will, determination, and the conscious mind. It is intelligent, logical, rational, and linear left-brained thinking.

Both of these can be seen within every aspect of creation and are typically present within the electrons and protons, as well. In case you want to achieve true success, you need to bring a balance between rational thinking and emotions. Through this balance, you can bring a significant pull of greatness toward you. Using this law, you can apply it to your routine and determine how you input it to the choices you make.

Adding a little bit of creative and emotional thinking to your decisions helps make more sense of it. In the end, it determines success by rationalizing your thoughts and situations and eventually making sure that your focus remains on a specific goal. Remember how we discussed indecisiveness among the major reasons for not achieving your life's goals? Well, this is one law that will cater to the issue and help you make a sound decision.

The Law of Compensation

This law dictates that your reward will be in direct proportion to your service; which is based on three principles. These principles are the need for what you do, your ability to do it, and the difficulty in replacing you.

The law of compensation is basically, *"you reap what you sow."* However, in this case, the compensation is not related to worldly gains, but rather, it's much different. Ralph Waldo Emerson talks about the law of compensation by saying that it is the essence of receiving precisely what you have done. If you do something that has a negative effect in the past, you will pay for it eventually; much like karma! In the case of 'reap and sow,' it can be seen as the law of overcompensation, where you receive the amount for the work you've done. If you've done more than the required amount, then your rewards are innumerable.

What you do need to know about this law is that it regularly also implies your gains based on the losses you have faced.

"For everything you have missed, you have gained something else; and for everything you gain, you lose something else."

-Ralph Waldo Emerson

It's evident that you can't receive anything without inputting even the slightest amount of effort, and more often than not, this effort is usually in terms of the losses that you face. It's quite simple really; you must be quite aware of how you absolutely cannot gain any benefits without undergoing some sort of pain. You have to make a small sacrifice for the greater betterment of your life. To understand this better, let's take an example, shall we?

This is a story I once heard about a man who won the lottery, simply through belief. Now this man was never really a firm believer of karma, and he wasn't such a great guy either. At this point, it's difficult to understand how the Law of Compensation relates to him, right? Well, according to the law, if he was a bad man, then he must face subsequent distress, but the universe works in mysterious ways. This man was adamant on staying at his roots and harming the lives of those around him. On the outside, to any layman, he was the definition of success; he had the biggest house, nice car, and great everything. One time, he happened to buy a lottery ticket, and as luck would have it, he won the lottery as well!

By now, it probably seems like he had everything in control, but he missed one great thing; the peace of mind. All his years of working smartly but wreaking havoc in the lives of others caught up with him in the cost of mental peace. No matter how much he had, nothing compared to the peace that he lost.

In the end, he hung himself a day after winning the lottery. Apparently, even the lottery couldn't save him from his conscience. From this, we learn that no matter what happens, the law of compensation will always catch up with you; no matter how successful, or poor others may find you to be.

The Law of Cause and Effect

This law is quite simple, and you can easily understand it if you pay attention. What it states is that every situation that comes by, and every action that occurs is not merely because of chance. It happens because of certain reasons or things that might have occurred. This world is built in an orderly fashion, and everything follows due to a reason. Therefore, if you have done something in hopes to gain a certain reward, you might just get it.

One of the things which is known to be a significant contribution of the 'chance' or 'coincidence' that occurs is your thoughts. We've discussed how vibrations are usually sent out into the universe, and that forms an attractive pull. Your thoughts become responsible for making you become a magnet for either positivity or negativity. This is often why it's said that you should always keep your thoughts in the direction of your goals and think positively.

Aligning thoughts is not always easy. However, you have to make sure that you send out the right energy to attract the right situation your way. As mentioned before, you might have remembered how I met DMX during one of my rides, and how, on another day, I got into an accident.

Those are the two contrasting examples of the impact of your thoughts on your everyday life. One of the biggest things that people tend to have an issue with is how they could change the cause and effect cycle. Well, it's actually quite easy! Through self-evaluation, you can gain an insight into where you're going wrong, and how you can fix it. How I worked to change my situation was easy; I took the time out to focus on why things had happened and how they had happened. Was it chance that I faced a car accident? Was it chance that made me meet my favorite rapper?

We already know that there is no such thing as chance. You are in charge of creating your own world and your own destiny. Everything that you did in the past matters, and what is in your mind now matters even more. This law will teach you to gain control; it's only through the control that you can succeed.

The Law of Oneness

Everyone is a part of the universe, and no two people are much different from one another. Regardless of how much you believe you're different from the next person there, it's essential to know that everyone is connected and have considerable similarities, even if none is apparent at all. It's probably also important to note that we also have a Divine connection with God in our own way as well. One of the most significant issues that people usually have when taking this law into consideration is; how is this connection going to benefit us in any way? Well, it's simple. We've seen the previous laws and how they've affected us. The law of oneness allows us to empathize and become the people we should be. This automatically brings forth enough goodness our way to have the law of compensation play its part.

Primarily, if I do good to someone else, the same thing would happen to me. There was once a video on social media where I saw the concept of *"carrying it forward."* This was also turned into a movie, which based itself on a fantastic life lesson. Carrying it forward was actually something good done by people for others, who then carry out more acts of kindness to someone else.

While it's all great for the subconscious mind, let's see how it affects you. There was a Malaysian advertisement on Facebook that gave me great insight into it. It began by showing a child begging for money to buy medicines for his mother. It just so happened that only one shop keeper was willing to help and gave him the money he needed.

Soon, it showed that several years passed, and the shopkeeper fell ill. He was admitted to the hospital, but his daughter didn't have enough funds to help him. It was then that his act of kindness toward the child years ago came back for him, as the child had grown to be the doctor operating on the shopkeeper. All the funds were forgiven, and the shopkeeper recovered.

This is a great example that shows just how much your actions can affect the circumstances in the future. Everything you do and think can come back to you one way or the other. The same is the case in terms of monetary growth as well. All you have to do is make sure you live a life of giving, and eventually, it will return to you as well.

The Law of Correspondence

The law of correspondence is something that is quite challenging for people to understand. Since it shows a particular aspect that is not often talked about frequently, people believe that it serves a purpose, which is not particularly as crucial as it's said. This law, however, is particular in defining the ultimate concept of self-understanding.

What the law of correspondence states is that, who you are on the inside is what will reflect on the outside, too. The reality is basically the mirror that shows your mental picture; if you believe in something, that's what you'll get. To gain a better understanding of this, let's take an example of your friends. This is one of the simplest ways to understand this law. More often than not, you might have heard how you pick friends who define you.

Sometimes they hurt you, but other times, they don't. Now, the friends you choose will basically be the people you think you deserve. If you hold an image of yourself a certain way, you'll find people who will treat you according to that image. Here, self-evaluation is the key to make sure you achieve greatness.

Ask yourself this; *"Am I a procrastinator?"* If you give a positive answer, then there's a more likely chance that you'll start acting on it as well. As they say, '*if you tell a lie long enough, it starts to sound true.*' That's how easily you can manipulate yourself. In circumstances where you find yourself unable to move forward toward your dreams, create an image inside of you that, if you were to look in the mirror, you would be satisfied with.

Think about this, we spend so much of our time trying to correct and beautify our physical selves; it's probably time that you did the same for your inner self as well. How else do you expect the law of correspondence and the law of compensation to work with you? You can will yourself to change your reality and also will yourself to succeed. I'm pretty sure some of the best scientists and authors like Napoleon Hill, faced defeat as well. It was their self-belief that allowed them to face the problems head-on and fix your issues.

Remember, positivity always starts from inside of you, and then you spread it out to the world.

The Law of Relativity

Have you heard of, *"one man's trash is another man's treasure?"* Well, that's what this law is about, in layman terms. It states that there is no such thing as good or bad; it's all relative. You can easily see this by defining your bad aspects. For instance, if you receive a gift which is far from what you were expecting; it's not really a good thing.

However, if someone else gets the same gift when they weren't expecting it, that's actually great.

Essentially, it's essential to realize that everything good or bad is a term that can be defined by only you. In that sense, having the freedom to define such an essential aspect in your life gives you the privilege of defining success as well. You can also put in Einstein's theory of relativity in here to determine your understanding. Einstein stated that everything is formulated in relation to something else. That means, there's always going to be a comparison.

This, in the case of the law of relativity, can be used positively. How? Well, if you make the right comparison, define the right graces, and take the right steps ahead, you can easily reach the path you're meant to be on. As mentioned before, only you define what is good or bad since everything is relative; you need to make sure that you recognize the graces coming your way. They're not always apparent, and they're not always what you would expect. You must have often heard, *"You don't know what you have unless you lose it."* This is the perfect example of that.

Taking things for granted is one of the top things that people have an issue with. If you have the potential to do something or even the resources, try not to waste them away. This is what can push you toward achieving your goals and finding the hidden potential in you. There was a time when I once saw the issues that came my way as something that beat me down to the punch. When I was at my lowest moments in life, I often looked back and noticed how I took even the slightest things for granted.

Imagine coming home to a clean house and a meal prepared for you; it might not sound like a big deal, but once you live on your own, you realize how lucky you used to be. Similarly, you can use your ability to make use of the most minor things you have and help them turn your failures into success. It may be a challenging start, but in the end, you realize that it's really not.

The Law of Vibration

This is one of the fundamental laws that you need to know, and it forms the crux of all the other laws, including the law of mentalism. Bob Proctor was the one who first introduced me to this insight, and it completely changed my life forever. It's something that will get you to start thinking as well. Everything is known to vibrate. It's primary science; everything is made of atoms, and atoms vibrate.

But what does this vibration have to do with your success? Well, it's easy. You know that everyone and everything is connected; it's the law of oneness. That means the universe also has a connection to you that not many people are aware of. What happens is that when you think, you don't realize the vibrations that you are sending out to the universe. It basically determines what you secretly want.

Now aligning your vibrations with your thoughts is not always easy. It can severely affect your ability to gain what you want. Keeping your ideas clear and precise will do the trick, or else the vibrations can significantly affect your chances of getting what you want. What you may call a 'coincidence,' as mentioned in the 'law of cause and effect' is the result of your vibrations coming back to you. In the previous chapters, we saw how much power your mind holds. Similarly, you need to understand just how it can affect your chances of success.

Vibrations are the things that can make your skin crawl, make you happy, make you scared, or feel emotions you have never felt before, simply through a place or person. This is usually because of the frequency that is attached to the place, object, or person. Even you have frequencies that can affect the people around you. However, in this particular case, let's see how your frequency determines your chances of receiving a particular thing.

Well, the frequency determines how much you want something. This is usually why I mentioned before that you need to keep thinking about what you need. If you think about owning a car and send out those vibrations, you will see how sooner or later, the situations would line up and you might end up owning a car. However, I also mentioned that you need to send out the RIGHT vibrations. This means your thoughts can also bring you the opposite of what you want if you're not clear enough.

The Law of Rhythm

This law states the rhythm of the world. Everything in this world has its own rhythm and works in its own time. You need to have patience and persistence to walk through the passage and receive what you have wanted to. Everything in this world, from the sun, the moon, the seasons, and even your feelings, move in a certain pattern. This pattern can easily be demonstrated by the pendulum.

Have you ever seen a pendulum at work? It consistently moves back and forth without a problem. In your case, you might notice a certain pattern in your feelings or situations. You must have had good days and even bad ones. However, according to a particular time, all of them have the tendency to pass and fade out on their own. Everything in this universe is destined at its own time, and this is a pattern that you might notice if you actually pay attention and think about it.

What this law basically states is that your good and bad days are based on a balance. Whether you like it or not, you have to go through it to gain insight toward a much bigger picture. It's similar to the law of gender; everything is created in a way to maintain balance in this life. The structures within the atoms or the opposing characters within you are all created so that nature can run its course with you. In the case of rhythm, you may not understand why bad things may happen to you, but through faith, you'll realize that they had to for the greater good.

I'm sure you don't believe me but let me give you an example; imagine that you had a flight, and it was crucial that you got on that very day, so as not to miss your friend's wedding. However, once you reach the airport, they wouldn't board the flight due to some discrepancies in your ticket. You're devastated because you miss your flight. However, once you reach home and turn on the television, you watch the news that the flight you were supposed to be on had crashed. If you had been on it, you wouldn't be a victim as well.

This is, in fact, a true story, and it shows how the rhythm of the universe aligns everything according to what is required for you at that time. Losing faith in this regard wouldn't get you anywhere, it would simply disrupt the vibrations that you send out to the universe. This is why the emphasis is always placed on making sure that you keep your hopes up and imagine looking at a much bigger picture. Every setback that you face renews your energy and gives you a much better perspective to move from.

For instance, let's say that you start a business. What might seem like a well-calculated plan ends up failing soon after you begin! In this case, the rhythm made you realize the flaws and where you may have gone wrong.

The Law of Gravity

Newton's law of gravitation is quite famous and states that everything has a gravitational force pulling it toward the earth. However, what does this law have to do with success? Well, it's simple, really. What happens is that the energy you send out to the universe pulls your desired goals toward you. Think back at the law of vibration; what did it state? It stated that your thoughts send out vibrations to the universe, and its frequencies determine the result of your life. Think about it; we mentioned that your subconscious mind is what makes you a magnet, and that means you are the point that pulls your desires toward you. How you go about doing that is entirely up to you. Well, let's say that I want cheesecake. I've craved it, pictured it, and even decided that I would make it myself if I didn't get it soon enough. However, the moment I was about to order a cheesecake, I opened the door to find it already ordered for me as a surprise from a friend.

I hadn't mentioned it to them or anything of that sort. However, it was randomly sent to me. This is an excellent example of gravitational energy working in terms of desires. The frequency of my desire was so strong, it sent it out to the universe, and the circumstances aligned in such a way that I received it. It was no coincidence; it was the universe rewarding me.

This law is something that works along with the law of vibration and forms the crux of all the laws of the universe. But here's an example of the wrong energy; if I hadn't specifically thought about the flavor of the cheesecake, I might have received a flavor that I didn't like. This would have ended in a disaster because, while I might have received something that I sought, it wasn't particularly the right type that I needed. In essence, this is one of the mistakes that people do. Thinking about something to the point of actually picturing it in front of you is definitely a great start, but it doesn't particularly mean that it will be what you truly desired unless you think about it the right way.

"Nothing in the world is worth having or worth doing unless it means effort, pain, difficulty... I have never in my life envied a human being who led an easy life. I have envied a great many people who led difficult lives and led them well."

Theodore Roosevelt

www.ingramcontent.com/pod-product-compliance
Lightning Source LLC
Chambersburg PA
CBHW021237090426
42740CB00006B/575